To Nate

Balance is what
we need

• Work
• Rest
• Worship
• Play

This Book has been
a real Blessing to
me — I hope it is
to you

Vaughn
Sept - 1990

The Rhythm of Life

The Rhythm of Life

by

RICHARD EXLEY

HONOR

A Division of Harrison House, Inc.
Tulsa, Oklahoma

Unless otherwise indicated,
all Scripture quotations are taken from
The Holy Bible: New International Version,
copyright © 1978 by the International Bible Society.
Used by permission of Zondervan Bible Publishers.

Cover photo: Scott Miller

The Rhythm of Life
ISBN 0-89274-469-3
Copyright © 1987 by Richard Exley
7807 E. 76th St.
Tulsa, Oklahoma 74133-3678

Published by Honor Books
A Division of Harrison House, Inc.
P. O. Box 35035
Tulsa, Oklahoma 74153

DEDICATION

To Roy Williams, a special friend whose vision for my ministry was often greater than my own.

CONTENTS

ACKNOWLEDGMENTS

I would like to express my deep gratitude to all of the people who gave of themselves to make this book possible.

To Dick and Irene Exley, my parents, whose lifelong love and marvelous example have made me whatever I am and whatever I may become.

To the Official Board and congregation of Christian Chapel, who so selflessly share their pastor, his time and energies, with the Kingdom. Without their support this book could not have been written.

To the Pastoral Staff at Christian Chapel, who took up the slack so I could be free to write, who not only believed in this project but who also encouraged me with their love and prayers.

To all the people at Harrison House, who have worked so diligently and with such faith to make *The Rhythm of Life* a reality. And to my wife, Brenda, my daughter, Leah, and her fiance, Todd, whose patience and support never cease to amaze me. They gave me time and space to write, listened when I wanted to read my day's work, encouraged me when I began to doubt myself, and always love me. Without all of you none of this would be possible.

The Rhythm of Life

INTRODUCTION

This is a book for people like me. Overachievers. Men and women who cannot rest as long as any task remains unfinished. We push ourselves in the pursuit of excellence. Some of us are visionaries pouring our lives into the work of the Kingdom. Some of us are simply ambitious or driven to succeed, driven to prove to ourselves and the world that we can do it, that we are somebody. Some of us are still trying to live up to our parents' unrealistic expectations, still searching for their approval and affirmation.

All of us, I'm afraid, are out of balance and suffering for it. We succeed, but experience only a momentary sense of success before the old emptiness returns. Noted author Harold Kushner writes, ". . . many apparently successful people (feel) that their success is undeserved and that one day people will unmask them for the frauds they are. For all the outward trappings of success, they feel hollow inside. They can never rest and enjoy their accomplishments. They need one new success after another. They need constant reassurance from the people around them to still the voice inside them that keeps saying, *If other people knew you the way I know you, they would know what a phony you are.*"[1]

Others find that their success is double-edged. Every benefit is offset by increased responsibilities. Now they work harder than ever just to keep up with the never ending demands. The pressure is relentless. There's no time for family or friends, no time for solitude or self. Even God is often crowded out.

These aren't bad people. In fact, they are often some of the finest people in the world. And it's their virtue, their goodness that is their undoing. Many ministers fall into this category, as do committed Christians and those involved in the various helping professions. Unfortunately, such apparent selfless service is often fueled by a desperate need to achieve, to be applauded. And the cost can be staggeringly high — an empty marriage, resentful children, burnout.

It's a subtle trap, a mindset masked in the work ethic. A Jewish rabbi alluded to it while addressing the graduating class of a rabbinic seminary. He told those young people about to embark on careers in the rabbinate, "There will be Friday evenings when you will rush your family through dinner so that you can get to services on time to give a sermon about the Sabbath as uninterrupted family time. There will be days when you will leave a sick child at home or a child studying for a test, while you go to teach religious values to the Temple youth group. There will be Sundays when you will cancel plans for a family picnic to officiate at a funeral, where you will praise the deceased as a man who never let his business interfere with his obligations to his family. And worst of all, you won't even realize what you are doing as you do it."[2]

That hits home, doesn't it? "And worst of all, you won't even realize what you are doing as you do it."[3]

I'm guilty. I've been there and I'll probably succumb again. But here's the good news: Once you recognize the symptoms and accept the solution, you'll usually catch yourself before you're in over your head. It happened to me just a few weeks ago. I wrote in my journal:

"Lord, forgive me —
I've failed You again.

"Some believers wouldn't consider it a failure,
but I know better.

"It's not prayerlessness, not this time.
Nor evil thoughts or vain imagination.
Or even unholy ambition.

"No, I've failed You in a much more subtle way.
I've become the ugliest of all things — a busy man.

"It was okay for a while.
The long hours,
   the constant pressure —
      counseling, administration, visitation —
         unrealistic expectations, relentless
            demands . . . .

"I loved what I was doing.
I was committed,
   creative,
      energetic . . . .
"Like a quick change artist
I switched hats,
   changed roles,
      tried to be all things to all people.

"There was no time for solitude or daydreaming.
Radio scripts had to be written,
   sermons prepared,
      deadlines met.

"It was exciting and demanding.
I was out to change the world.

"But there was no rhythm in my life,
no balance between work and rest, worship and play.

"Now I'm not just a busy man.
I'm an angry man too.
I'm tempted to resent the people I love
and to dread the ministry I'm committed to.

"Forgive me, Lord,
for working too hard and playing far too little.
Let me become a child again
at least for a time each day.

"Balance my busyness with solitude,
my work with rest.
Let me walk away from time to time
so I can return refreshed and renewed.

"Help me, Lord, for I am a busy man."

Apparently, Jesus Himself struggled with these very issues, at least the gospels seem to suggest He did. Dr. David L. McKenna, President of Asbury Theological Seminary and author of several books, commenting on Mark 3:7 says, "Jesus withdraws to the sea with His disciples in order to regain His balance in the rhythm of life. During His ministry in Galilee, the rhythm has been reduced to constant work with little rest, and even less opportunity for worship and play. In fact, when He goes to the synagogues for worship, He meets either human need that requires work or spiritual hardness that requires contest. Worship and work may have become so intermingled that Jesus senses the potential loss of the effective edge in His work and the fine-tuning of His communion with God. In modern terms, He might have been on the borderline of 'executive burn-out' . . . . His withdrawal to the sea is not cowardice (or laziness), it is a credit to His intuitive sense that the time has come for rest and play.

"Work is an activity of high intensity and high production. But as God set the example, even creative work must be balanced by a period of 'rest,' when physical energies are restored in order to work again. Worship and play, then, must be added to the work/rest cycle in order to fulfill the finer hungers of persons who are created in the image of God."[4]

He goes on to say, "Modern society has upset the rhythm of life. Work has been devalued and play has been invaded by the purpose of work. With so much leisure and so many options, play

14

has been subjected to a time-clock schedule with its demand for successful production. In many instances, worship has been eliminated from the rhythm of life and rest has become a dreaded experience on a 'crash pad.' The result is that work is a necessary evil, play is work, worship is idolatry and rest is a short course in death.''[5]

It doesn't have to be like that, life doesn't have to be a rat race. I believe all of that can be turned around. I believe work can be meaningful, rest can renew, worship can inspire, and play can be the joyous pleasure that seasons it all. That's why I wrote this book.

Take a minute and think about it. Are you practicing the rhythm of life, that delicate balance between work and rest, worship and play? Are you fulfilled? Are the most important relationships in your life all they should be? Do you take time for yourself? For God? What about play? Are you fun to live with? These are just some of the issues we'll be dealing with as we try to implement principles which will enable us to live life to the very fullest in the truest sense.

The Rhythm of Life is more than just a book to be read. It's an invitation to laugh and cry, to feel the deepest and most profound feelings that you are capable of experiencing. Before long you'll pause, put your fingers between the pages, and relive a treasured experience. By the time you've finished this book, it will be more yours than mine — a collage, a reflection of your personal history.

Footnotes

1. Harold Kushner, *When All You've Ever Wanted Isn't Enough* (New York: Summit Books — a Division of Simon and Schuster, Inc., 1986), p. 4.

2. Ibid., p. 10.

3. Ibid., p. 10.

4. David L. McKenna, *The Communicator's Commentary: Mark* (Waco: Word Books, 1982), p. 77.

5. Ibid., p. 77.

Part I

WORK

Part I

WORK

Work is neither inherently good nor evil, moral nor immoral. It's what we make it. Some people worship their work, sacrificing everything — family, friends, even their own personhood — at the altar of ambition. Tragically, they are often the last to recognize that they have become a driven person. Blindly they plunge ahead, oblivious to their own obsession. If they manage to avoid executive burnout, they frequently end up successful, but alone.

At the other end of the spectrum is the counterculture of the hippies. The middle to late sixties and early seventies were times of dramatic change in American life. The adolescents who came of age were frequently the products of a materialistic home where the father was away on business much of the time, and the mother, a socialite of sorts, was equally committed to numerous activities outside the home. Disillusioned by the resulting emptiness and unhappiness, this generation determined not to let their lives be governed by the same unfulfilling materialistic values.

Instead, they determined to "find themselves," to "do their own thing." Unfortunately, the only thing that really changed was the strategy, the plan. Underneath, they were still motivated by the same self-seeking desires. They recognized the futility of seeking fulfillment through success and the things it could buy, but they were blind to the emptiness of living a life with no higher goal than self-actualization. Their path was different from that of their parents and "the establishment," but it ended in the same inner desolation. The enemy wasn't work, but motive.

Between these extremes is the called man. The one who sees himself as a steward, his life as a gift to be invested and managed for the Lifegiver, and his work as an expression of who he is. For him, work is its own reward. It's an important part of his life, but only a part. He's obedient rather than ambitious, committed rather than competitive. For him, nothing is more important than pleasing the One Who called him. Consequently he is free to balance his work with rest, worship and play.

Chapter 1

THE ACHIEVER SYNDROME

The other day someone mailed me a comic strip called "Cathy." The first frame shows Cathy standing by her desk as a group of co-workers begin filing in from lunch. She asks, "Did you have a good lunch?" and immediately wishes she hadn't. The first guy responds, "Fantastic! I did a forty minute workout and a three mile swim!"

A lady executive says, "I dictated all my correspondence in the jacuzzi!"

"I studied my French language tapes on the stationary cycle!" chimes in a secretary.

A yuppie-type adds, "I hit my heart rate target zone and endorphin peak while meeting with my broker on side-by-side rowing machines!"

The last frame pictures Cathy alone at her desk with a look of chagrin. Wistfully she asks, "Whatever happened to the good old days when 'Having a good lunch' meant you got to eat something?"[1]

What a commentary on our times. We Americans are obsessed with busyness. Even our "leisure" time is dominated with the need to be productive. No wonder William McNamara, author of *The Art of Being Human* and *The Human Adventure: Contemplation for Every Man,* concluded, "Possibly the greatest malaise in our country today is our neurotic compulsion to work."[2] We are driven to succeed, to get ahead, to get established in our careers. Any temptation toward moderation is quickly swallowed up by guilt. Life is competitive. Our performance is being measured against that of our peers. We can't let up, not even for a moment, or life will pass us by.

We are Americans, and we have been taught that all things are possible to him who works hard. And not only possible, but expected! We are competitive — may the best man win. We are haunted by self-doubt and work all the harder because of it, driven by the mistaken assumption that success will still those tormenting voices within. The illusion of fulfillment calls us to redouble our efforts and so we forge ahead — blindly, desperately. Soon we define our lives by what we do: We're a banker, or a teacher, or a plumber. Tragically, we have lost our way, our identity. We have become workaholics.

You may be wondering how you can tell if you are a workaholic or just a conscientious person. Let me give you a quick checkup.

— Is work the primary source of your identity? If you were suddenly unemployed, would you still know who you are? Would you still be a person of worth?

— Do you believe work is inherently good, and therefore the more work you do, the better person you are? When you're "tooting your own horn" do you "bemoan" the long hours you work? If you do, the chances are that you ascribe to this tenet, at least unconsciously.

— Do you feel you are not really serving the Lord unless you consistently push to the point of fatigue? Do you ascribe to the old tenet that you would rather burn out than rust out?

— Do you think the more you work, the more God loves you? Let me put it a different way. When you imagine standing before the Lord on Judgment Day, in what do you place your confidence? In what you've done for Him or in what He's done for you?

— Do you feel indispensable? Think about it. What would happen if you couldn't work for several weeks?

— Do you control your work or does it control you? Do you work in order to make a living or do you live to work?

If you answered "yes" to more than three of those questions, you need to take a serious look at your priorities. Work is too important in your life! If you're not already a workaholic, you are probably well on your way to becoming one.

Let me give you the profile of a workaholic. Gordon MacDonald, past president of Intervarsity Christian Fellowship and long-time pastor, calls him a driven person and writes, "There are lots of driven people doing very good things. Driven people are not necessarily bad folk, although the consequences of their drivenness may produce unfortunate results. In fact, driven people often make great contributions. They start organizations; they provide jobs and opportunities; they are often very bright and offer ways and means of doing things that benefit many other people. But nevertheless they are driven, and one worries about their ability to sustain the pace without danger to themselves."[3]

MacDonald lists eight recognizable characteristics.

"— 1) A driven person is most often gratified only by accomplishment . . . So the driven person begins to look for ways to accumulate more and more achievements . . . He becomes the sort of person who is always reading books and attending seminars that promise to help him to use what time he has even more effectively. Why? So that he can produce more accomplishments, which in turn will provide greater gratification.

"— 2) A driven person is preoccupied with the symbols of accomplishment . . . That means that he will be aware of the symbols of status: titles, office size and location, positions on organizational charts, and special privileges.

"— 3) A driven person is usually caught in the uncontrolled pursuit of expansion. Driven people like to be a part of something that is getting bigger and more successful . . . They rarely have any time to appreciate the achievements to date.

"— 4) Driven people tend to have a limited regard for integrity . . . Shortcuts to success become a way of life. Because the goal is so important, they drift into ethical shabbiness. Driven people become frighteningly pragmatic.

"— 5) Driven people often possess limited or undeveloped people skills . . . There is usually a 'trail of bodies' in the wake of the driven person. Of this person we are most likely to find ourselves saying, 'He is miserable to work with, but he certainly gets things done.'

"— 6) Driven people tend to be highly competitive . . . Thus, he is likely to see others as competitors or as enemies who must be beaten — perhaps even humiliated — in the process.

"— 7) A driven person often possesses a volcanic force of anger.

"— 8) Driven people are usually abnormally busy. They are usually too busy for the pursuit of ordinary relationships in marriage, family, or friendship, . . . not to speak of one with God."[4]

As we've already noted, driven people, or workaholics, often make great contributions. They start organizations; they provide jobs and opportunities; they are often very bright and offer ways and means of doing things that are beneficial to many. But, at what cost? Because they have not balanced their work with rest, worship and play, they are terribly vulnerable.

Life's meaningfulness often escapes them. They achieve success without experiencing fulfillment! For them, hell is the loneliness of having everything and knowing that it is still not enough. Or as Oscar Wilde so succinctly put it, "In this world there are only two tragedies. One is not getting what one wants, and the other is getting it."[5]

Gail Sheehy, author of the best-seller *Passages*, coined the phrase "concomitant growth" to describe the unique challenge of adulthood.[6] She uses it to explain the adult's need to develop concurrently on what she identifies as the three basic frontiers of his life: work or vocation, relationships with significant others, and one's own unique selfhood, the realm of inwardness, that part of one's self that is expressed simply for one's own private delight. I would add a fourth dimension — the spiritual, one's relationship with God. That's a tall order. However, we ignore it to our own peril. Without concomitant growth, we become prime candidates for a mid-life crisis.

According to Daniel Levinson, author of *The Seasons of A Man's Life*, "There are many different interpretations of this phenomenon, but, generally speaking, it is a time in life — usually occurring between the late 30's and the late 50's — when people go through a great deal of turmoil and difficulty in their work, their marriage or their dealings with their children. It's a time when people question seriously their life patterns and goals."[7]

I think it's safe to conclude that this crisis is attributable, at least in part, to our tendency to over-invest in one or the other of these areas in our earlier years. The effects of this imbalance begin to surface sometime in our middle years. For example, the workaholic pours almost all of his energy into his career and thus has little or no life apart from his work. When he begins to realize that work is not enough, that he needs something more than "success" to fulfill him, he often experiences a mid-life crisis.

Gail Sheehy; whose book, *Passages*, is the standard by which all other works on the subject are judged; tells of a forty-six-year-old TV newscaster who had climbed to the top of his profession and was basking in the affluence and affirmation that went with being a national celebrity. However, he was not as satisfied or fulfilled as one might suppose. He commented one day: "I am near the top of the mountain that I saw as a young man, but lo and behold, this is not snow up here, it is mostly salt." He said most of the persons he knew who were considered "successful" had left their personal lives far behind them. Professionally, they were terrific, but on a personal level their lives were in utter disarray.[8]

Harold Kushner further documents this unfortunate syndrome with this personal observation: "In the last few years, I have found myself traveling and lecturing a great deal. I have spoken in some thirty-eight states and six foreign countries. Often I am invited to the home of some prominent member of the community for dinner before my lecture, or for a reception afterward. Most of the time, my hosts are very gracious and the gatherings enjoyable. But every now and then I find myself uncomfortable in that setting, and one evening I finally realized why. Some people have to be very competitive to reach the top, and once they have gotten there, they find it hard to break the habit of competitiveness. They are not able to relax and chat with me. They feel that they have to impress me by telling me how successful they are, by dropping the names of important people they know. Sometimes they start an intellectual argument with me, trying to show me that they know more about my subject than I do. On those occasions, I find myself wondering why they feel they have to be so competitive, why they have to respond to a guest in their home as a competitor-to-be-challenged, and whether part of the price they have paid for their success, part of their bargain with the devil if you will, is that they keep transforming friends into enemies."[9]

The teacher who penned Ecclesiastes may have been just such a man, a workaholic. He wrote: "I undertook great projects: I built houses for myself and planted vineyards. I made gardens and parks and planted all kinds of fruit trees in them. I made reservoirs . . . I also owned more herds and flocks than anyone in Jerusalem before me. I amassed silver and gold for myself . . . I became greater by far than anyone in Jerusalem before me . . . I denied myself nothing my eyes desired; I refused my heart no pleasure.

"Yet when I surveyed all that my hands had done and what I had toiled to achieve, everything was meaningless, a chasing after the wind . . . I hated all the things I had toiled for under the sun . . . my heart began to despair over all my toilsome labor . . . all . . . [my] . . . work is pain and grief; even at night . . . [my] . . . mind does not rest. This too is meaningless" (Eccl. 2:4-11,18,20,23).

What happened? He achieved success, but he did not experience fulfillment. He established a great kingdom, but he had no one to share it with. "He makes me think of Howard Hughes and Lyndon Johnson in their last years, experts at manipulating people to do their will, masters of the art of exercising power, yet they ended up lonely old men surrounded by hired servants and favor seekers, wondering why so few people loved them."[10]

Not every workaholic will be so successful, but you can be assured they will all experience the same exasperating sense of futility. The more the workaholic achieves, the more biting, the more bitter his futility. There is not enough success, power, or wealth in the world to satisfy the human heart's hunger for relationships. Unfortunately, most driven people never realize this or at least not until they have severely jeopardized the significant relationships in their lives.

They not only achieve success without experiencing fulfillment, but they also have been known to *sacrifice everything — family, friends, even their own personhood, on the altar of ambition.* Usually it is not a conscious decision. In fact, they become very adept at self-deception and rationalize that they are doing it for their family.

Naively, the church world has often believed themselves immune. Surely, we reason, no Christian would be so self-serving, so obviously ambitious. Unfortunately, we Christians are made of the same stuff as other men, and we too are tempted to live our lives in the desperate pursuit of material things, career advancement, and the obvious power and recognition it affords. Such "success," however, is not without its price.

The first casualty is frequently the family. "Overcommitment is the number one marriage killer," according to Dr. James Dobson, prolific author on family relationships. He reasons, "How can a man and woman communicate with each other when they're too worn out even to talk? How can they pray together when every moment is programmed to the limit? How can they enjoy a sexual relationship when they are exhausted at the end of every day? How can they 'date' one another or take walks in the rain or sit by a fire when they face the tyranny of an unfinished 'to do' list?"[11]

How indeed? He concludes, "We have deluded ourselves into believing that circumstances have forced us to work too hard for a short time, when, in fact, we are driven from within. We lack the discipline to limit our entanglements with the world, choosing instead to be dominated by our work and the materialistic gadgetry it will bring. And what is sacrificed in the process are the loving relationships with wives and children and friends who give life meaning."[12]

Nor is the clergy immune. They too are driven to excel. And in their relentless pursuit of achievement, they often fall prey to the same materialism which inundates the workaday world, howbeit a religious version. Success often replaces service as the motivating factor, and they frequently get caught up in the numbers game — attendance, membership, budgets, and building programs. When this happens, the church is no longer a community, but a religious conglomerate; the minister is no longer really a shepherd, a pastor, but just the chief executive officer. Like many of his secular counterparts, he may become a power broker, sacrificing family and friends on the altar of his misdirected ambition.

The price he pays is extravagantly high, although the ultimate cost may not be obvious for a quarter-century or more. Ultimately his inner emptiness, his emotional and spiritual void will demand a resolution. By now he's probably achieved more "success" than he ever dreamed possible, and with it, more frustration. This isn't how he's supposed to feel. Where's the fulfillment, the satisfaction? Who is there to share his achievements? He is not intimate with his wife, not even close, and his children are strangers, grown and gone, making a life of their own.

If his public ministry is any indication of his work habits, then it's safe to conclude that he is a confirmed workaholic who thinks nothing of putting in eighty to ninety hours a week. Suddenly, at mid-life, he realizes the futility of it all, but he's at a loss to make a change. He doesn't know anything else. Lonely and depressed, he's especially vulnerable.

It's not hard to imagine what happens next. In the course of his pastoral duties, he finds himself counseling with an estranged wife. Her inner emptiness mirrors his own, and, almost without realizing it, an emotional bond is formed. For the first time in longer than he can remember, he feels alive. Here's a woman who appreciates him as a man, as a person. She listens to him and really cares about the things he's feeling.

At this point he probably would be shocked if someone suggested he was well on his way to having an affair. He's never allowed that thought to enter his mind — well, almost never. Dr. Carlfred Broderick, successful marriage counselor, has talked with dozens of couples who have been fully committed to fidelity, yet found themselves involved in affairs. He says:

"I am convinced that more people get themselves into the pain of infidelity through empathy, concern and compassion than through any base motive. The world is full of lonely and vulnerable people, hungry for a sympathetic ear and a shoulder to cry on. With a little help from rationalization, the sympathy leads smoothly into tenderness, the tenderness to the need for privacy, the privacy to physical consolation, and the consolation straight to bed."[13]

H. Norman Wright; pastor, professor, therapist and author of 45 books; says, "The need for emotional intimacy is one of the greatest reasons for the affair."[14] Peter Kreitler and Bill Bruns concur. They write in *Affair Prevention:*

"Affairs begin not just for sexual reasons but to satisfy the basic need we all have for closeness, goodness, kindness, togetherness — what I call the 'ness' needs. When these needs are not met on a regular basis in a marriage, the motivation may be to find a person who will be good to us, touch us, hold us, give us a feeling of closeness. Sexual fulfillment may indeed become an important part of an extramarital relationship, but the 'ness' needs are, for most men and women I know, initially more important."[15]

What am I trying to say? Simply this: When we worship our work at the sacrifice of everything else, we are setting ourselves up for some devastating losses in our personal lives. Even if we never have an affair, or if we have one but our spouse never finds out, we are still the losers. As one marriage counselor said, "Most marriages that fail never end up in the divorce court." What good is a family if you're not a "family"? And what good is success if you have no one to share it with?

A famous banker was given a testimonial dinner and presented a distinguished award. He expressed his appreciation, then said, "It doesn't mean much to me now. You see my wife died last year, and I have no one to share it with."

So it is with the workaholic. He may achieve great "success," but he won't have anyone to share it with. Even if his spouse hasn't died, and his marriage hasn't ended in divorce, he still won't have anyone to share it with. Relationships require time and tenderness, communication and closeness. The workaholic has neither the time nor interest. Consequently, he frequently ends up a lonely and bitter man.

For years I read Ecclesiastes with a mixture of frustration and confusion. Why, I wondered, was it even included in the Bible? It was the most depressing thing I had ever read. Then one day its meaning dawned on me. The writer was a workaholic nearing the end of his days. He had invested his life in his career rather than relationships and now, too late, he realizes the utter futility of a life lived for things rather than people.

He was successful — "I became greater by far than anyone in Jerusalem before me" (Eccl. 2:9). — But he found no pleasure or fulfillment. ". . . I hated life, because the work that is done under the sun was grievous to me. All of it is meaningless, a chasing after the wind" (Eccl. 2:17).

And at the end of his life, he realized he had no one to whom he wanted to leave his wealth. Though he had fathered many children, they were all strangers to him. "I hated all the things I had toiled for under the sun, because I must leave them to the one who comes after me. And who knows whether he will be a wise man or a fool? Yet he will have control over all the work into which I have poured my effort and skill under the sun. This too is meaningless" (Eccl. 2:18,19).

As we come to the close of this chapter, let me ask you some hard questions. Are you living the kind of life that will leave you fulfilled when you near the end of your earthly existence? To my knowledge no one has ever said on his deathbed, "I wish I had spent more time on my business." Are you investing time, love and energy in your spouse and your children? Do they get priority time or just the scraps you have left after giving your best in the marketplace?

No one can set your priorities for you, only you can do that. In order to do it well, you will have to decide what is really important and then commit yourself to it at all costs. Dr. James Dobson makes an eloquent case for relationships in *Straight Talk to Men and Their Wives*. He writes, "I have concluded that the accumulation of wealth, even if I could achieve it, is an insufficient reason for living. When I reach the end of my days, a moment or two from now, I must look backward on something more meaningful than the pursuit of houses and land and machines and stocks and bonds. Nor is fame of any lasting benefit. I will consider my earthly existence to have been wasted unless I can recall a loving family, a consistent investment in the lives of people, and an earnest attempt to serve the God Who made me. Nothing else makes much sense."[16]

Footnotes

1. Cathy Guisewite, "Cathy" (1987 United Press Syndicate), *The Tulsa World*, 3 Mar. 1987.

2. William McNamara, "Wasting Time Creatively" (cassette tape), Spiritual Life Institute, Star Route One, Sedona, Arizona.

3. Gordon MacDonald, *Ordering Your Private World* (Nashville: Published by a division of Thomas Nelson, 1984), p. 31.

4. Ibid., pp. 31-36.

5. Kushner, p. 3.

6. Gail Sheehy, quoted in *Stages* by John Claypool (Waco: Word Books, 1977), p. 60.

7. "Midlife Crisis — Is It Avoidable?" Interview with Daniel J. Levinson, psychologist, *U.S. News & World Report,* 25 Oct. 1982, p. 73.

8. Claypool, *Stages*, pp. 60,61.

9. Kushner, p. 39.

10. Ibid., p. 34.

11. James C. Dobson, *Straight Talk to Men and Their Wives* (Waco: Word Books, 1980), p. 136.

12. Ibid., p. 139.

13. Carlfred Broderick, *Couples* (New York: Simon and Schuster, Inc., 1979), p. 163.

14. H. Norman Wright, *Seasons of a Marriage* (Ventura: Regal Books — A Division of Gospel Light Publications, 1982), p. 111.

15. Peter Kreitler with Bill Bruns, *Affair Prevention* (New York: Macmillan Publishing Co., 1981), p. 68.

16. Dobson, p. 148.

Chapter 2

WORK ISN'T THE ENEMY

I'm a product of the sixties. I vividly remember the Cuban Missile Crisis, the assassination of President John F. Kennedy, civil rights marches, student demonstrations and the Vietnam War. We entered the decade with a certain innocence. There were no problems that couldn't be solved with dedication and technology. Jack Kennedy was our Camelot, the Peace Corps our conscience. The Bay of Pigs was the first crack in our dream world. Then came the assassinations of the Kennedy brothers — John and Robert — followed by that of Dr. Martin Luther King, Jr. Finally the big one — Vietnam.

My generation lost its innocence almost overnight. We entered the sixties with nothing on our minds more serious than the senior prom, a white sport coat and a pink carnation. Vietnam changed all of that, and I watched in disbelief as our country suffered its deepest division since the War Between the States a century earlier.

With an enthusiasm matched only by their naivete, my generation took to the streets in peace marches, protests and other demonstrations. Initially, I believe they truly thought they could change the system, that "love" and "peace" would prevail. They had seen the results of the American Dream — on a personal level: a nice house in the suburbs, two cars, an absentee father, a working mother, and more than enough unhappiness to go around. On the national and international level, it produced pollution, exploitation, the Cold War, the draft and Vietnam. In their minds there had to be a better way, though it was never quite clear what that "better way" was to be. At least it wasn't clear to those of us who were on the outside looking in.

Since they couldn't change the system, many of them decided to drop out. They rejected the values of their parents. Material things were not important. Success, status, wealth and power were meaningless, as far as they were concerned. All that mattered was their personal happiness. They were determined to "find themselves," to "get their head together," to "do their own thing."

Their quest took a variety of forms. Some of them formed communes and lived off the land. Others turned to various eastern religions, while some tried the occult. Almost all of them experimented with drugs at least occasionally. And to their chagrin, they discovered the same old emptiness that haunted the world of their workaholic parents. They were asking the right questions, but still coming up with the wrong answers.

They watched their parents and their parents' friends become workaholics and — for what? It seemed the more successful they became, the less meaning they had in their lives. The psychiatrist Rollo May describes such a person in *Man's Search for Himself:* "The clearest picture of the empty life is the suburban man, who gets up at the same hour every weekday morning, takes the same train to work in the city, performs the same task at the office, lunches at the same place, leaves the same tip for the waitress each day, comes home on the same train each night, and has 2.3 children, goes to church every Christmas and Easter, and moves through a routine mechanical existence year after year until he finally retires at sixty-five and very soon thereafter dies of heart failure."[1] May adds, "I've always had the secret suspicion, however, that he dies of boredom!"[2]

The counterculturists mistakenly concluded that the problem was work. Either a man sold out to his work and became a workaholic or he became trapped in a deadly routine. In either case, his life and his relationships lacked meaning. There's probably some truth to that, but it is a half truth at best. Since we've already examined the workaholic, let's turn our attention to May's "suburban man." Some jobs are demeaning, to be sure, but more often than not, the problem lies with the person more than the job. If a person believes in himself and in the value of the work he is doing, then even the most pedestrian task can be meaningful.

An experience Anthony Campolo, author of *You Can Make A Difference,* had while visiting Scotland is a case in point. He and his wife wanted to visit the shipyards where her grandfather had worked before the family immigrated to America. They asked directions of a middle-aged woman who informed them that she was at that very moment on her way to her job at the shipyard and would be glad to take them there personally.

Campolo writes, "On our way we passed numerous shipbuilders who had just finished their work on the daytime shift. Each of them bid an enthusiastic greeting to our new friend. Everybody we passed knew her by name and she, likewise, knew everyone we encountered. There was a funloving quality about her personality, and her whole demeanor communicated that she was enjoying life.

" 'What's your job at the shipyard?' I asked. She stopped in her tracks, took my arm, and then spoke to me in such a way that I was sure she was about to tell me something of enormous importance.

" 'What do I do?' she asked rhetorically. 'What do I do?' she asked a second time, as if I had not caught the question the first time. 'I'm the one who cleans the ships.' And then, obviously impressed with the importance of her task, she added, 'And you know, nary a ship goes to sea until I say it's clean enough. It's my job to see to it that every bit of dirt is polished away. That's what I do.' "[3]

It's hard for me to imagine a person with an attitude like that living an empty life or dying of boredom. Her attitude, her enthusiasm for her work, gave her task dignity and her life meaning. She's an unusual creature, no doubt, a throwback to an earlier time when a person's work was an extension of himself and not just a job to do. Surely she deserves some further attention.

Anything I write about her attitude and the impact it may have had on her life and personhood is purely subjective speculation. I know nothing about her except what Campolo wrote. Still, I believe some cautious speculation may be in order, so indulge me. And, as we look at her attitude toward work, let's consider our own as well.

Apparently she took pride in her work, not because it was prestigious, but because she recognized herself as a person of value. Therefore, anything she invested herself in took on proportionate worth. Instead of looking for her self-esteem in her work, she imparted a sense of value to everything she did. We could conclude that she did not feel good about her work simply because it was important in, and of, itself. Rather, her work was important because she was doing it.

Compare her attitude with that of the workaholic who sees his work as a means to an end — a way of earning money, making a name for himself, even a way of exercising power. He sees all of these things as proof of his personhood. Unfortunately it's a losing battle. There is not enough success in the world to quiet the discordant voices within. Self-esteem is not the by-product of achievement, but the natural consequence of a healthy relationship with one's parents, peers and, of course, God. It is a matter of who you are, not what you have done.

Compare this woman's attitude with the hippie of the sixties and early seventies who was interested primarily in personal fulfillment. For him, work was only important if it contributed to his

inner journey of self-discovery and self-expression. I realize that
I am being simplistic. There are those who would argue that the
counterculture was the moral conscience of a capitalistic society,
that they were the ones who cared enough to challenge the system
and demand reform. There may have been an element of truth
in that at one point. However, I think history bears me out when
I say that social concerns soon gave way to the more pedestrian
matters of self-actualization. Those who took to the streets
demonstrating for peace in Vietnam and social justice at home
soon gave up their moral indignation to seek personal peace and
a private utopia. They forsook our cities in droves to seek their
own version of the American Dream. They established communes,
determined to live the simple life.

On the surface, there is something appealing about a rustic
lifestyle. Who among us hasn't longed for the simpler times of
"Walton's Mountain" or the carefree days pictured in the Coke
commercials of a decade ago. You know the ones — where a fresh-
faced girl gets out of a cab and runs through a field of shoulder
high corn toward the farmhouse of her youth. On the porch is her
dad in his bib overalls and denim shirt with the sleeves rolled up
above his elbows. Her mother steps out the front door, wiping her
hands on her apron, just in time to see the girl run into her daddy's
strong arms. It's the homecoming we've all dreamed of, the simple
life of our fantasies, and Coke capitalized on those innate longings.

In reality, I wonder if there was ever a time like that, or if
it has always been just a nostalgic memory, a yearning of the heart.
Most of us can indulge those fleeting feelings for a few minutes
and then return to present reality. Apparently the counterculturist
of the sixties and seventies could not. When the simpler, communal
lifestyle proved to be haunted with the same old jealousies and
insecurities which inhabited the middle-class, workaday world of
his parents, he often turned to drugs in a misdirected attempt to
escape the reality of his emptiness.

On the surface, this search for self-fulfillment with its repudiation of materialism seems right and good, almost noble. On closer

examination it proves to be just another disguise for the same old self-serving attitude. The driven man invests his whole life in his work in a desperate search for success and the fulfillment it's supposed to bring. The counterculturist drops out for the same ignoble reason. He, too, is on the same desperate journey in search of fulfillment. He has just taken a different path.

The hippies of the late sixties and early seventies have become the yuppies of the eighties. What happened to all their idealism, all their brave rhetoric? It turned out to be just that. It was a pipe dream. The repudiation of materialism, with its creature comforts and status symbols, doesn't ensure the fulfillment we all seek any more than does the accumulation of wealth and the achievement of status. In the final analysis, it might be argued that if one is going to be empty and unfulfilled, he might as well do it while living in a comfortable house and driving a BMW. After all, there is nothing inherently noble about poverty or the suffering that generally accompanies it.

Are we to conclude then, like the writer of Ecclesiastes, that "Everything is meaningless . . ." (Eccl. 1:2) "Utterly meaningless!"? That "All things are wearisome, more than one can say" (Eccl. 1:8)? Do we cry as he did, "What a heavy burden God has laid on men! . . . what does he [man] gain, since he toils for the wind? All his days he eats in darkness, with great frustration, affliction and anger" (Eccl. 1:13; 5:16,17)?

No! There is another option. Between the driven man and the dropout is the called man. The one who sees himself as a steward, his life as a gift to be invested and managed for the Lifegiver, and his work as an expression of who he is. For him, work is its own reward. It's an important part of his life, but only a part. He's obedient rather than ambitious, committed rather than competitive. Nothing is more important than pleasing the One Who called him and, as a consequence, he is free to balance his work with rest, worship and play.

Footnotes

1. Rollo May, quoted in *The Splendor of Easter,* Floyd W. Thatcher (Waco: Word Books, 1980), pp. 56,57.

2. Ibid., p. 56.

3. Anthony Campolo, *Who Switched the Price Tags?* (Waco: Word Books, 1986), p. 88.

Chapter 3

FINDING FULFILLMENT

I like to work. I really do. For a long time, I've been a little ashamed to say that. After all, I'm a product of the sixties, and I've been warned about materialism and burnout for years. I think I understand the futility of a life built on work and work alone. I've seen the consequences of executive burnout: nerves rubbed raw, angry outbursts, inappropriate emotional responses, and the inability to make decisions. Still, the truth of the matter is that I like to work. I agree with Solomon who said, ". . . when God . . . enables him [any man] . . . to accept his lot and be happy in his work — this is a gift of God" (Eccl. 5:19).

There's nothing in life more meaningful than working with God in the reconstruction of a shattered life. Some people call that *counseling.* I call it *ministry,* and it's always been a team effort among the three of us — God, the person and myself. Preaching is great, too. Not just the actual event, but the whole process. Waiting before the Lord, researching the Scriptures, preparing the material and, of course, preaching it. In short, I enjoy becoming the instrument that God uses to speak to His people.

Don't misunderstand me. I didn't say my work was easy or painless. I said it was meaningful. In truth, the ministry is tremendously demanding (as I am sure your work is, as well). Expectations are unrealistically high, the hours are often long, human need is almost overwhelming, and the work is never done. Sometimes the best of us feel in-over-our-heads. When it happens to me, you can usually read about it in my journal.

"I'm tired, Lord.
Bone weary from the inside out.

"I'm tired of a constantly cluttered desk
and an overcrowded calendar.

"I'm tired of broken things,
like marriages with too little love,
and families with too much anger.

"I'm tired of problems I can't solve,
and hurts I can't heal.
I'm tired of deadlines and decisions —
duties done without any pleasure.

"I'm tired, Lord.
I really am."

Another time I wrote:

"Lord,
My creative juices are at a low ebb.

"I have no inspiration,
  no insight,
    no freshness.

"It's been sometime now
since I felt truly alive.

"I can't remember
the last time I walked barefoot in the park,
or lay on my back in the grass watching the clouds,

or sat in my study at night
with only a kerosene lamp for light,
thinking of Grandma Miller
and the good times we had.

"I'm homesick for the mountains,
    for the smell of pines after a rain,
        for the sound of the wind in the aspens.

"I'm hungry for home-baked bread and country cream,
    home-canned peaches,
        and fresh tomatoes right off the vine.

"I'm so tired of books
which satiate my mind,
without touching my soul.

"I want to feel.
I want to laugh and cry.
    I want to live life to the fullest.
        I want to love, and be loved.

"Forgive me, Lord.
Sometimes I get so caught up in my work,
    I miss life's best.

"Remind me
to balance my busyness with rest, worship and
play."

You may be thinking, "Of course, he enjoys his work. He has a meaningful job with high visibility and lots of positive strokes. Let him put in fifty hours a week in the sweat shop where I work, and then he can talk to me about job satisfaction."

I can understand how you would feel that way, but in all fairness I must point out that there are hundreds of ministers who receive little, or no, job satisfaction. My sense of fulfillment has more to do with who I am than what I do. I feel good about my work because I feel good about myself. As a consequence, I've liked every job I've ever had; some more than others, of course. As an enterprising junior high student, I hustled yard jobs. In high school, I worked 35 hours a week cutting donuts in a bakery. While attending Bible college, I was a janitor in a large warehouse. At various other times, I stacked hay in eastern Colorado, worked on the docks at the Port of Houston and sold new cars. I'll be the first to admit that none of them provided the job satisfaction that I've found in the ministry. I did, however, find fulfillment of one kind or another in each one of them.

You don't have to be miserable and unfulfilled. You too can find satisfaction in your work. With few exceptions, you won't have to change anything except your attitude and your theology of work.

Work is not a consequence of man's fall, nor part of the curse, as many of us have been taught to believe. We are created in the image of God, and He is a creative workman, a master craftsman. As beings made in His likeness, we are designed to share in His work and His world. Genesis 2:15 says: "The Lord God took the man and put him in the Garden of Eden to *work* it . . . ."

Arthur Gordon, author of *A Touch of Wonder*, once asked a friend in the ministry the secret of self-renewal. The pastor smiled and replied, "Give in to goodness now and then. I don't mean masochistic self-sacrifice. I mean the deliberate performance of an act that has ethical value: helping someone in need, righting a wrong, forgiving an enemy. For best results, the act should be one that can't possibly benefit you."

"This leads to self-renewal?" Gordon asked.

"Why not? Since we live in an ethical universe, the performance of ethical acts must align us with the forces that sustain it. So, if we give in to goodness once in a while, we gain strength. If we consistently refuse, we're at cross-purposes with everything, including our deepest nature. People not only have the capacity for ethical behavior, they have a built-in need for it. If you give in to goodness reasonably often, you won't have to seek self-renewal. It will come to you."[1]

Now apply that principle to work. People not only have the capacity for meaningful work, they have a built-in need for it. When we realize this and approach our work as an opportunity to align ourselves with the Creator and His Creation, we position ourselves to be fulfilled. Any other attitude puts us at cross-purposes with everything, including our deepest nature. Therefore, the first tenet in our theology of work is: *Work is an expression of who we are, an expression of the creative nature we share with God.* This truth sanctifies and gives dignity to even the most mundane task.

Next, we need to examine our reasons for working. What are your motives? Why do you work? Max Lerner, author of *The Age of Overkill: A Preface To World Politics,* said, "I like to get paid for my work, but what fulfills me and makes me whole is the work, not the payment. I am involved with both, but if I am to be a whole person, I must know what is primary for me, and what is secondary. If I know that the quality and integrity of my work come first, then I am true to my profession both as writer and as teacher. If money comes first, then I am corrupt — even if I never steal anything or accept a bribe. If I am unsure about which comes first, then I am morally confused and a divided person."[2]

That pretty well says it, doesn't it? All of us work for a variety of reasons. If we want to be fulfilled, we had better know what reasons are primary, and what reasons are secondary. We work to make a living, to provide for our families. We work in order to be successful, to get recognition and to gain security. There's nothing wrong with that as long as those are secondary motives. Lerner put it so succinctly, "I like to get paid for my work, but what fulfills me and makes me whole is the work, not the payment." In other words, work is its own reward.

I remember when this truth first began to dawn on me. For years, I had sought the approval and affirmation of both my family and friends. I literally inundated them with the details of my ministry. My need for their approval was insatiable. No matter what they said, it wasn't enough. I wanted more — always more. In my desperation, I even went so far as to subtly alter the facts in order to present myself in the most advantageous light. I had to be better than everyone else, and my family and friends had to recognize it. As you can imagine, I made life miserable for all of us.

Things didn't change overnight. In fact, it was a process spanning several years, and continues even now. It started when I realized I couldn't compete. In the ministry, a man's success or importance is often measured by the numbers — membership, baptisms, budget and building programs.

I struck out on all counts. For the first fourteen years of ministry, I pastored small churches (under 100 members) in out-of-the-way places. In desperation, I took my sagging self-esteem to God. In His presence I began to discover a new way of determining my self-worth. Instead of the numbers game, over which I had only the slightest control, I realized I could base my success on my relationship with Him. I set new goals — character goals, spiritual goals. I measured myself, not against other ministers, but by my potential Christlikeness.

Since this new standard was inward and private, rather than public, I noticed an immediate decrease in the monologues about "my ministry." Proportionately, I realized a slackening in my need for public approval. For the first time I began to examine what it was that truly brought me satisfaction. I discovered, much to my surprise, that it was the act of ministry, not the recognition I had so avidly sought.

It was still nice to receive affirmation from others. I will probably always enjoy it when someone says, "Pastor, that message really spoke to me." But more and more, I came to understand that my deepest joy comes from the act of ministry itself, and from the approval of my heavenly Father. Nothing anyone can say will ever equal the feeling of aliveness that exists during the actual preaching experience. To know that God has chosen to speak through me, and to witness the transformation which the Living Word brings to men and women is all the reward I really need.

Let me emphasize again that the ministry is not the only work God is in. In fact, all work is sacred when the worker is in right relationship with Him. A childhood experience shared by Anthony Campolo in *Who Switched the Price Tags?* is a case in point:

"When I was a boy, my father worked at the RCA factory located in Camden, New Jersey. His wages were so low that it could be said that he was exploited. My father was a cabinet-maker back in the days when cabinets for radios were made by hand. While he worked for starvation wages, he did get something from his job that was more important than money. He got psychic gratification from his work. Making those cabinets was a real 'turn-on' for him. He felt alive when he fashioned things of beauty out of wood. For him, what he produced was an extension of his ego. There was something mystical that he imparted to each cabinet he built. In a strange way, they were *his* cabinets. He would not get the profits from constructing them. He would not be given the recognition which he deserved for his craftsmanship. But he got something more — much more.

"When we did our family visiting, which in the pre-TV era was a major form of entertainment, Dad would look for the radio in the house. If there was a console that was of his vintage, I would be given the responsibility of investigating. It was my assignment to get behind that big upright console and see if my father's initials were inscribed on it. My dad always initialed the back side of the cabinets he built. After all, they were his cabinets. He had made them. On two different occasions, I came across his initials, and when I did, he basked in self-satisfaction. And I had the feeling that I had the most creative, ingenious father in the world. My father had fun making radio cabinets. He had fun looking at the work of his hands."[3]

The second tenet then in our theology of work is: *All work is sacred when the worker is in right relationship with the Creator. And the joy of work is its own reward.*

When a man enjoys his work, as the elder Campolo obviously did, and when he maintains the rhythm of life, his work will be renewing even if it is time-consuming, mentally taxing, or physically demanding. The secret is finding a yoke that fits.

Some weeks ago, I was preaching a sermon on rest that renews, based on our Lord's invitation recorded in Matthew 11:28-30. Jesus said, " 'Come to me, all you who are weary and burdened, and I will give you rest. Take my yoke upon you and learn from me, for I am gentle and humble in heart, and you will find rest for your souls. For my yoke is easy and my burden is light.' "

The point I was trying to make is that rest without meaningful work is not rest at all, but boredom. It is not renewing. Rather than restoring us, it makes us lethargic. That's why Jesus invites us to take His yoke and learn of Him. He specializes in yokes that fit. He has an amazing ability to match the man with the job, the person with the position. In fact, one of the ways to determine if you are in God's will, is to see how well your yoke fits, how renewing your work is for you.

Notice I said it is one of the ways for determining God's will, not necessarily the ultimate test, and certainly not the only one. Vocationally, you may be exactly where God wants you, doing exactly what He's called you to do and still burn out. The problem is not the "yoke," but the fact that you haven't practiced the rhythm of life — that delicate balance between work and rest, worship and play. Many wonderful people have crashed and burned, been lost to the Kingdom, for this very reason.

Others are unfulfilled because they have the wrong attitude.

"A new worker at a factory asked his shop steward what it was like to work in this factory. The shop steward answered with a question of his own: 'What was it like at your last job?' 'Oh,' said the new worker, 'it was a miserable job. I didn't like the work and the bosses were unfair to me.' 'Unfortunately,' responded the shop steward, 'you'll find it much the same here.'

"Later, another new worker asked the same shop steward exactly the same question. Once again the steward responded with his own question, 'What was it like at your last job?' 'Oh,' said the new worker, 'it was wonderful. The work was interesting, everybody was good to me. The working conditions were ideal.' 'Well,' said the shop steward, 'I'm happy to report that you will find this place just as wonderful as the last place where you worked.' "[4]

The point of this little parable should be readily obvious. A person's attitude often determines his experience. Around our house we've adopted a little rhyme to remind us:

"Two men looked out
through prison bars.
One man saw the mud,
one man saw the stars!"

It's often just a matter of perspective. Before you consider changing jobs in hopes of finding the fulfillment you seek, examine your attitude. If it's not right, then it doesn't matter where you work, what you're paid or even what you do. If your attitude is wrong, you will always be unhappy. By the same token, if it's right, you'll be able to say with the apostle Paul, ". . . I have learned the secret of being content in any and every situation . . . whether living in plenty or in want" (Phil. 4:12).

Now, back to my original point. How well does your yoke fit? Are your gifts and abilities matched to your work? If not, then you are probably pretty frustrated.

Let me illustrate. When time permits, I enjoy tinkering around the house. On occasion I have been known to build a bookcase, and out of necessity, I've even remodeled a parsonage or two. Still, working with my hands is not my forte. I'm not a craftsman. If I had to spend my life as a cabinetmaker, I would be frustrated indeed. Every project would simply remind me that I had two left hands. After a while, I would either conclude that I was a real klutz, or I would chafe under the restrains of a job that inhibited my true talents.

How, you may be wondering, does a person discover what they are good at? The first clue is pleasure. Most of us enjoy doing what we do well. I call it "going with the flow," "doing what comes natural." Unfortunately, we can't always provide for ourselves by doing those things, so we may have to look deeper. The second clue is desire. What do I want to do? Most people, left to their own intuition, will gravitate to their areas of giftedness. And, finally, many of us must learn by trial and error.

Arthur Gordon relates a personal experience which is a good case-in-point. He had taken a job, selling insurance I believe, to pay for his college education. Things hadn't worked out, and just before the holiday break, he quit his job. His entire time at home was tainted with the shame of his failure. He put off telling his father until the night before he had to return for the new semester.

"Nothing," he writes, "is so indelible as the memory of (that) failure. I remember how the coal fire muttered in the grate, and the tawny light flickered on the shadowy bookcases. I said slowly, 'I'm a terrible salesman. I get self-conscious and discouraged. Other people do the job much better. I'm in the wrong pew, that's all.'

"I waited for the remonstrance, the exhortation, the you-can-do-it-if-you-really-try lecture. But the room remained silent. Finally, my father laughed gently. 'Well,' he said, 'that's fine. It's just as important to learn what you can't do as what you can. Now let's forget about that and talk about getting you into the right pew!' "[5]

That's great, isn't it? Unfortunately, experiences like that are far too rare. Consequently, many people spend a lifetime in the "wrong pew." Because they are afraid to own up to their mistake and make a new start, they never know the joy of renewing work, work which fulfills them. And sometimes it wasn't a mistake, but a vocation that was designed just for a certain season in their life.

I had such an experience about two years ago. For about twelve years, pastoral counseling was a major part of my ministry. I spent between fifteen and twenty hours each week in scheduled sessions.

It was tiring, it was exhausting, but it was also renewing. Seeing broken lives restored, past hurts healed, and shattered marriages renewed was fulfilling in ways I can't even describe. Being part of that redemptive process was more meaningful than I can ever say. Even though the hours were long, the pressure heavy, somehow I exulted in it. It was regenerating to my spirit — it renewed me! Balanced with rest, worship and play, it wore well.

Then things started to change. Our church was experiencing significant growth with all the accompanying change. We were in a building program, adding new staff, and expanding our ministries. My own ministry was expanding as well. I was traveling and ministering throughout the United States with ever-increasing frequency. The radio ministry was requiring more and more time. Soon, I began to resent every request for counseling. Each session was a major challenge. God gave us grace, and people continued to receive ministry, but it was sucking the life right out of me.

It took me almost two years and a close brush with burnout to realize what was happening. God was changing my ministry, giving me a new yoke, but I was still trying to wear the old one. The counseling no longer fulfilled me, it was no longer an investment which renewed me, but an expenditure — one which depleted me.

Always remember when you are doing God's work in God's time, it is an investment from which you will get personal returns. When you try to wear a yoke that no longer fits, you become depleted because your investments have turned into expenditures. It will suck the life right out of you, too.

The third tenet in our theology of work then is: *Find a yoke that fits and wear it.* Make sure your attitude is right, make sure you have a servant's heart. Then match your skills and temperament with your life's vocation.

"One day when Christopher Wren, the English architect, was directing the construction of St. Paul's Cathedral in London, he stopped to talk to one of the laborers at the building site. 'What do you do?' Wren inquired of the man. Not realizing that he was talking to the great architect, the man, who was a cement mixer, answered, 'Sir, can't you see? I'm building a great cathedral.' "[6]

I like that! Here was a man who saw past the limits of his job description to the grand scheme and was able to claim it as his own. He wasn't just mixing cement, he was building a beautiful cathedral. It was more than a job, more than a way of making a living. It was an opportunity to be part of something great, and he had sense enough to know it.

The fourth tenet in our theology of work then is: *We are co-laborers with God.* We are working with Him to feed, clothe and shelter His human family. We share His dream for a world where poverty, disease, injustice and unrighteousness have been obliterated. He is the eternal architect, we are just the cement mixers. Still there's something grand about working with Him. It gives my life's work meaning and eternal value.

I am convinced that God intends for us to enjoy our work and the fruit of our labors. At least, that's what the teacher of Ecclesiastes concluded. He wrote, ". . . I realized that it is good and proper for a man to eat and drink, and to find satisfaction in his toilsome labor . . . I know that there is nothing better for men than to be happy and do good while they live. That every man may eat and drink, and find satisfaction in all his toil — this is the gift of God . . . (Such a man) seldom reflects on the days of his life, because God keeps him occupied with gladness of heart" (Eccl. 5:18; 3:12,13; 5:20).

Remember, if you make the accumulation of wealth, or the pursuit of happiness, or any other personal benefit the goal of your labors, you will find only futility. But, if you give yourself selflessly in service to God and others, God Himself will give you the desires of your heart. Fulfillment is not a goal. It is the consequence of a life lived in rhythm with God!

Footnotes

1. Arthur Gordon, *A Touch of Wonder* (Old Tappan: Fleming H. Revell Company, 1974), pp. 102,103.

2. Max Lerner quoted in *The Relational Revolution* by Bruce Larson (Waco: Word Books, 1976), p. 133.

3. Campolo, pp. 106,107.

4. Ibid., pp. 109,110.

5. Gordon, pp. 92,93.

6. Campolo, p. 111.

Part II

REST

Part II

REST

Rest has gotten a bad rap. How many times have you heard someone say, "I wish my body didn't require sleep. It seems like such a waste"? Maybe you've even said it yourself. I know I have. After all, we are active people with a "production" mentality. Our lives are geared to goods and services. Our culture admires the doers and shakers. If you can work 80 to 90 hours a week, serve on various civic boards, remain active in your church and get by on five to six hours of sleep a night, you are held in high esteem.

But, who gives a rip about rest? Who ever heard of giving someone a pat on the back for having sense enough to take it easy? Yet, rest is just as important, just as necessary, as work. Is it going too far to suggest that much of the current stress-related illness and the general decline in mental health has its roots right here, in our total disregard for rest?

Remember, rest was God's idea. He thought it up and called it the Sabbath. It limited travel and entertainment, and prohibited work on the seventh day of every week. Most of us busy-beaver types tend to view the Sabbath principle as an outdated, legalistic imposition. Nothing could be further from the truth. The Sabbath is God's gift of rest, a reward at the end of a demanding week of hard work.

Rest is more than a good night's sleep, more than mere physical recuperation. It's a time when we forget our problems and life's pressing demands long enough to remember who we are. It's a few minutes of solitude in the midst of a hectic day. A time when we pause in the mad busyness of living and remember a special moment from the past. This kind of rest, taken daily or at least regularly, restores our physical being and renews our emotional and spiritual energies.

Chapter 4

RISK, REST AND RENEWAL

"In January, 1959, a thirty-two-year-old disc jockey named Peter Tripp staged a 200-hour 'wake-a-thon' in a Times Square booth for the benefit of the March of Dimes. During this sleepless marathon, he was attended by several doctors and given periodic medical examinations, performance tests, and psychological tests. From the beginning, Tripp had to fight to keep himself from falling asleep. After two days, he began to have hallucinations, such as seeing cobwebs in his shoes. By 100 hours, his memory was becoming quite poor, and he was having a great deal of difficulty with simple performance tests. His hallucinations became more and more frightening: he saw a doctor's tweed suit as a suit of furry worms. When he went to a nearby hotel for a change of clothing, he saw the bureau drawer in flames. To explain these visions to himself, he decided that the fire had been deliberately set by the doctors in order to frighten and test him.

"A simple algebra problem that he had earlier solved with ease now required such superhuman effort that Tripp broke down, frightened at his inability to solve the problem, fighting to perform. Scientists saw the spectacle of a suave New York radio entertainer trying vainly to find his way through the alphabet.

"After 170 hours the agony had become almost unbearable to watch. At times Tripp was no longer sure he was himself, and frequently tried to gain proof of his identity. Although he behaved as if he were awake, his brain wave patterns resembled those of sleep. In his psychotic delusion, he was convinced that the doctors were in a conspiracy against him to send him to jail . . . At the end of the 200 sleepless hours, nightmare, hallucination and reality had merged, and he felt he was the victim of a sadistic conspiracy among the doctors."[1]

I share the Peter Tripp story to illustrate what we are doing to ourselves when we continually violate the rhythm of rest. When we burn the candle at both ends, we are not only depleting our physical energies, but risking our spiritual and emotional wholeness as well. Like Tripp, we can probably justify our hectic schedule — it's for a good cause, it's only for a little while. When I finish this project, when I graduate, when I . . .

Don't deceive yourself. Rest is not optional. It can't wait! "Six days you shall labor, but on the seventh day you shall rest; even during the plowing season and harvest you must rest" (Ex. 34:21). Plowing season and harvest were absolutely critical to the life cycle of an agrarian culture. A single day could spell the difference between feast and famine. Still God said, ". . . you must rest" (Ex. 34:21).

In Old Testament times, Sabbath-breakers were executed. Exodus 35:2 says, ". . . Whoever does any work on it [the Sabbath] must be put to death." Those who break the Sabbath today suffer the same consequences. Not at the hands of a religious or judicial system but as an inevitable consequence of their transgression. When we violate the Sabbath principle of rest, our souls suffer as do our relationships, our creative energies and, ultimately, our physical health.

This truth was driven home to me almost two years ago. For more than a year I had ignored the Sabbath. I hadn't taken a day off. I knew it was wrong, but there seemed to be one emergency after another, not to mention the ever-present demands of a growing congregation. I was preaching five and six times a week, leading a Field Education reflection group at Oral Roberts University, continuing a heavy counseling load, and hosting a live 90-minute, call-in radio program weekly. We were just completing a major building program at our church and, on top of everything else, my father had open-heart surgery followed three weeks later (to the day) by an emergency gall bladder operation.

Physically and emotionally, I was drained, more than I realized. I began to resent my work, especially the counseling with its constant requirement to be affirming and encouraging. I told someone I felt like a piece of raw meat in a tank of piranhas. For a while I thought I could work myself through it. I mean, what choice did I have? If I tried to take a few days off, the work just piled up. It was always waiting for me when I got back. Besides, I had been away from the church as much as I dared during my father's illness.

By and large I managed to minister with surprising proficiency. On the inside, though, I was falling apart. My nerves were rubbed raw. I had no spiritual or emotional reserves left. My wife and daughter received the brunt of my angry outbursts. Things finally came to a head on Labor Day. I just lost control, screamed at Brenda over nothing, then I hated myself.

My brother, Bob, and his wife were spending the weekend with us and I found myself expressing my pent-up feelings to him. Once I started to talk, I couldn't seem to stop. I was tired, but there was no time to rest. I loved my work, but it was killing me. I felt trapped and hated that feeling, too. By now I was crying — I couldn't stop. All the pain I had kept under such careful control just came pouring out. It scared me. It really did. I hadn't realized just how close to the edge I was.

With Bob's help, I was able to make some important decisions. First, I had to admit that I wasn't a superman. I couldn't do it all. Then I had to decide what to do, what to delegate, and what to let go undone. Finally, I had to return to the rhythm of rest, had to take my day off religiously.

The emotional release that outburst afforded me was invaluable. However, it would have been of little lasting benefit without the subsequent lifestyle change. I'm learning to live within my emotional limits. Just as I have to budget my finances in order to live within my means, so must I budget my emotional and spiritual resources as well. If I give out more than I take in, I become overdrawn. By practicing the Sabbath principle of rest and solitude, I am able to make regular deposits and return to my public ministry with renewed energy and effectiveness. In addition, I'm a much better husband and father, as well as a more satisfied man.

As Richard Foster writes in *The Freedom of Simplicity,* "After a certain amount of immersion in public life, I begin to burn out. And I have noticed that I burn out inwardly long before I do outwardly. Hence, I must be careful not to become a frantic bundle of hollow energy, busy among people but devoid of life. I must learn when to retreat, like Jesus, and experience the recreating power of God . . . And along our journey we need to discover numerous 'tarrying places' where we can receive heavenly manna."[2]

You don't have to be a corporate executive or a busy minister to burn out. It can happen to anyone who doesn't practice the rhythm of life. Several years ago I heard Charles Blair, the pastor of Calvary Temple in Denver, Colorado, tell a touching story which illustrates the cumulative effect of life's unending demands.

It happened late one afternoon as he was leaving the church parking lot at the end of a demanding day. As he turned onto the street, he caught sight of a woman sitting at the bus stop, alone and weeping. He circled the block, parked the car and made his way to her. Introducing himself, he asked if she was all right. His concern obviously embarrassed her. She hastily dried her tears and said, "Yes, I'm fine. Just tired, that's all. Really tired."

She went on to tell him that she got up every morning at 5:30 — fixed breakfast and made lunches for her husband and children.

After she got her husband off to work and the kids off to school, she tidied up the house a bit. Then she caught the bus which took her across town where she spent the day cleaning houses. Late each afternoon she took another bus home, arriving just in time to fix supper. Then there was laundry to do, and homework the kids needed help with, leaving no time for herself. Generally, around midnight, she would collapse into bed for a few hours of exhausted sleep only to arise the next morning to do it all over again.

She was okay — just weary in well-doing — a little disillusioned with her life, perhaps, and wondering whatever happened to her dreams, guilty for feeling that way since she had such an obviously hardworking husband and such good kids.

Does that sound familiar? Oh, you may have to modify the circumstances just a bit, but I think most of us can identify with her weariness and her guilt. Like her, we are blessed. But, that doesn't seem to keep us from wearing out. It's usually not the biggies that get us but life's little hangnails. Those daily demands that just won't go away. Or as one country philosopher put it, "The thing about life is, it's so daily!"

What can she do? How can she incorporate rest, worship and play into her already overscheduled life? That's a good question, but I'm not sure it's the right one for us to ask. The question that demands an answer from us, the one that we must answer is: "What am I going to do? What practical and specific steps will I take to restore rhythm to my life?"

From my perspective, there are two major hindrances prohibiting rest. The first is psychological. Most of us, subconsciously at least, think of rest as a waste, a weakness. That's a big hurdle to get over in a society which emphasizes physical prowess and the bottom line. No one wants to be seen as a nonproductive malingerer. Noted author Judith Viorst catches the essence of our obsession in a piece called "Self-improvement Program."

"I've finished six pillows in Needlepoint,
And I'm reading Jane Austen and Kant,
And I'm up to the pork with black beans in Advanced
Chinese Cooking.
I don't have to struggle to find myself
For I already know what I want.
I want to be healthy and wise and extremely
good-looking.

"I'm learning new glazes in Pottery Class,
And I'm playing new chords in Guitar,
And in Yoga I'm starting to master the lotus
position.
I don't have to ponder priorities
For I already know what they are:
To be good-looking, healthy, and wise.
And adored in addition.

"I'm improving my serve with a tennis pro,
And I'm practicing verb forms in Greek,
And in Primal Scream Therapy all my frustrations
are vented.

"I don't have to ask what I'm searching for
Since I already know that I seek
To be good-looking, healthy, and wise.
And adored.
And contented.

"I've bloomed in Organic Gardening,
And in Dance I have tightened my thighs,
And in Consciousness Raising there's no one around
who can top me.
And I'm working all day and I'm working all night
To be good-looking, healthy, and wise.
And adored.
And contented.
And brave.

And well-read.
And a marvelous hostess, . . .
And bilingual,
Athletic,
Artistic . . . Won't someone please stop me?"[3]

That's a little exaggerated, of course, but it does reflect the tremendous pressure we are under to perform, to measure up. To a person trapped in the self-improvement mind-set, rest is almost blasphemous. It's a waste, it's laziness! Nonsense. Rest is a gift from God. It's a reward after a full day of productive labor. Besides, it's absolutely essential to spiritual and emotional wholeness, not to say anything about physical well-being.

The second hurdle is habit, lifestyle. Most of us are over-extended and overcommitted. Incorporating quality rest into our hectic routine will require some major lifestyle changes, affecting not only ourselves and our immediate family, but also those with whom we work, worship and socialize.

Before we can intelligently change our lifestyle, we must clarify our values. We must decide what things are really important to us. Erma Bombeck, the housewife's philosopher, writes:

"Someone asked me the other day if I had my life to live over would I change anything? My answer was no, but then I thought about it and changed my mind. If I had my life to live over again I would have waxed less and listened more. I would never have insisted the car windows be rolled up on a summer day because my hair had just been teased and sprayed. I would have invited friends over to dinner, even if the carpet was stained and the sofa faded. I would have eaten popcorn in the good living room and worried less about the dirt when you lit the fireplace. I would have taken time to listen to my grandfather ramble about his youth. I would have burnt the pink candle sculptured like a rose before it melted while being stored. I would have sat cross-legged on the lawn with my children and never worried about the grass stains. I would have cried and laughed less while watching television and more while watching real life. I would have eaten less cottage cheese and more ice cream. I would have gone to bed when I was sick instead of pretending the earth would go into a holding pattern if I weren't there for the day. I would never have bought anything just because it was practical, wouldn't show soil and was guaranteed to last a lifetime. When my child kissed me impetuously I would never have said, 'Later, now go wash up for dinner.' There would have been more 'I love you's,' more 'I'm sorry's,' more 'I'm listenings' but mostly given another shot at life I would seize every minute of it, look at it and really see it, try it on, live it, exhaust it, and never give the minute back until there was nothing left of it."[4]

That, I believe, reflects the sentiments of the masses. Given a second chance, most of us would like to think that we would do better, that we would invest more in relationships, and less in things. Perhaps, although I have my doubts. Anyway, the real question isn't, "What would I do if I had my life to live over?" but "What am I going to do with the rest of my life? Do I have the courage to change? Do I know how to change?"

In *The Freedom of Simplicity,* Richard Foster suggests: "(That) we keep a record of all our activities for one month. Then we should rank them in the following way: absolutely essential — #1, important but not essential — #2, helpful but not necessary — #3, trivial — #4. Next, we must ruthlessly eliminate all of the last two categories and 20 percent of the first two."[5] He then concludes, "We are too busy only because we want to be too busy. We could cut out a great deal of our activity and not seriously affect our productivity."[6]

I couldn't agree more, but I'm afraid many of us don't know the difference between what is absolutely essential and what is trivial. And it's virtually impossible to establish priorities without one absolute, one governing principle. Foster explains it like this:

"Within all of us is a whole conglomerate of selves. There is the timid self, the courageous self, the business self, the parental self, the religious self, the literary self, the energetic self. And all of these selves are rugged individualists. No bargaining or compromise for them. Each one screams to protect his or her vested interests. If a decision is made to spend a relaxed evening listening to Chopin, the business self and the civic self rise up in protest at the loss of precious time. The energetic self paces back and forth impatient and frustrated, and the religious self reminds us of the lost opportunities for study or evangelistic contact. If the decision is to accept an appointment on the human services board, the civic self smiles with satisfaction, but all the excluded selves filibuster. No wonder we feel distracted and torn. No wonder we overcommit our schedules and live lives of frantic faithfulness. But when we experience life at the Center, all is changed. Our many selves come under the unifying control of the divine Arbitrator. No longer are we forced to live by an inner majority rule which always leaves a disgruntled minority. The divine Yes or No settles all minority reports. Everything becomes oriented to this new Center of reference. The quiet evening can be enjoyed to the fullest because our many selves have been stilled by the Holy Within. The business self, the religious self, the energetic self, all are at peace because they know we are living in obedience. There is no need to wave the flag of self-interest, since all things good and needful will be given their proper attention at the appropriate time. We enter a refreshing balance and equilibrium in life."[7]

When our lives are lived from the Divine Center, work and rest, worship and play all have equal importance, and all are given appropriate priority. In addition, much unnecessary stress can be eliminated by recognizing our individual work/rest cycles and working within them. For instance, my work day is divided into two parts. I arise each workday morning at 5:15 and drive to the church for prayer between 6:00 and 7:00. This is followed by a vigorous game of racquetball, and I am back in the office by 8:45. My mornings are devoted to pastoral duties, administrative details, and my radio broadcasts. I have a working lunch, and then I go home around 3 P.M.

As soon as I get home, I take a short nap and then begin my second work day which is devoted to writing. The nap serves not only to rejuvenate my energies, but also helps to clear my mind of the day's activities so I can come to my writing as fresh as possible.

Within each workday, I have also developed routines which minimize day-to-day decisions. On Tuesdays, we have a staff meeting. I write my weekly column for the church newsletter, dictate correspondence and deal with a host of little details. On Wednesday mornings, I have appointments and work on my Wednesday evening message. Thursdays are devoted to radio. Fridays are writing days, and on Saturday I prepare for Sunday. Of course, there are constant interruptions, life is unpredictable you know, but for the most part, that is an accurate overview of my week. By doing the same chore on the same day each week, I develop a flow. It also eliminates the emotional energy I would otherwise spend trying to decide what to do and where to start.

We all have limited amounts of time and energy so we must use them wisely. The less emotional energy we spend on routine tasks, the more there is to invest in the things that really matter. By recognizing and developing your own work/rest cycle you minimize your emotional expenditures while maximizing your effectiveness. This leaves more time and energy for the other areas of your life — your relationships, your spiritual life and your inner self.

To develop a rhythm of rest in a work-oriented society is demanding indeed, but the benefits more than justify the effort. In the next two chapters we will explore a theology of rest, and I will share some practical steps for incorporating rest in a hectic life.

Footnotes

1. Floyd L. Ruch and Philip G. Zimbardo, *Psychology And Life,* 8th Ed. (Glenview: Scott, Foresman and Company, 1971), p. 260.

2. Richard Foster, *The Freedom of Simplicity* (San Francisco: Harper & Row, 1981), p. 91.

3. Judith Viorst, *How Did I Get To Be 40 & Other Atrocities* (New York: Simon and Schuster, Inc., 1978), p. 45.

4. Erma Bombeck, *At Wit's End* (1981 Field Enterprises Inc., Field Newspaper Syndicate).

5. Foster, pp. 91,92.

6. Ibid., p. 92.

7. Ibid., pp. 80,81.

Chapter 5

A RECREATIVE EXPERIENCE

I'm the kind of person who accepts almost nothing at face value. Therefore, when the Scriptures say, "Observe the Sabbath day . . ." (Deut. 5:12), I want to know why. Why is it holy? Why is it different from any other day? Why would God command His people not to work, not to be productive on the seventh day? It's not disrespect that makes me question everything, but curiosity — a holy curiosity, if you will allow me to be so presumptuous. If I understand the reasoning behind the commandment, it is much easier for me to incorporate it into my behavior.

The Old Testament doesn't really address this issue except to say that in six days the Lord made the heavens and the earth and He rested on the seventh day. Therefore, the Sabbath day is holy (see Ex. 20:11). Deuteronomy 5:15 says, "Remember that you were slaves in Egypt and that the Lord your God brought you out of there with a mighty hand and an outstretched arm. Therefore the Lord your God has commanded you to observe the Sabbath day."

Apparently God is saying that once a week He wants His people to pause in the busyness of living and remember that He is their Creator and Deliverer. In light of the hostile environment (i.e., famine and plagues) and the constant threat from alien armies, it's easy to appreciate Israel's need for such a reminder. It served to reassure them of God's special provision and protection. In short, the Sabbath wasn't for God's benefit, but theirs.

In addition to serving as a constant reminder of mankind's special relationship to the Creator, it also legitimized rest and reaffirmed the value of relationships. Alan Goldberg, associate professor of counseling and guidance at Syracuse University, writes: "Although introduced by the lighting of the candles and sanctified by the recitation of the kiddush over a cup of wine, the Sabbath is not distinguished by or identified primarily with unique ritual symbols. Instead, its holiness rests in its emphasis on time — time for interpersonal relationships, for reestablishing contact with the world of nature, for the expression of the emotional dimensions of being, and for the enjoyment of the present. On the Sabbath everyday activities and weekly routines are put aside and time is made for oneself, one's family, and one's friends."[1]

The Sabbath begins at sundown on Friday and all preparations are to be completed ahead of time so the Sabbath can be totally free of mundane concerns. The tensions and conflicts of the week are to be put aside so it can be enjoyed. According to Goldberg: "Friday evening traditionally is spent at home with family and friends, thus providing a regular opportunity for family members to become reacquainted with one another and their neighbors . . . The prohibitions against riding, the use of money, and work serve to keep everyone within the boundaries of the neighborhood and to encourage socializing, contemplation, study, dialogue, and those activities that promote refreshment and personal renewal."[2]

Worship also is an essential part of the Sabbath. I have deliberately not discussed it, however, because it is beyond the scope of this chapter. At this time we are focusing on rest and its importance to our well-being — emotional, spiritual and physical. The Sabbath, with its severe restrictions on work and travel, is not an archaic imposition, as most of us assume, nor a hair shirt, but a gift from a wise and loving God.

In our culture, work has become a god. It is the preeminent factor in organizing human life and establishing personal identities. It so dominates people's lives that there is little time for themselves or their families. The Sabbath is God's answer. It serves as a counterbalance establishing the inalienable human right to rest. It is designed to protect us from the dangers of physical exhaustion, psychological stress and the interpersonal alienation which results from idolization and overidentification with work.

For centuries, the Christian Church continued to practice the principle of the Sabbath, although they observed the first day of the week instead of the seventh in honor of the Lord's resurrection. World War II changed all of that with the first widespread practice of seven-day-a-week, twenty-four-hour-a-day production. By the sixties and seventies, retailers were following suit, and the Sabbath principle was a thing of the past. Not coincidentally, there was a significant increase in emotional dysfunction, juvenile delinquency and divorce. Without the rhythm of rest provided by the Sabbath, life was unraveling at the seams.

While I contend for the Sabbath, I am not naive enough to think that we can return to a legalistic observance of it. Rather, I am talking about the Sabbath principle where we recognize and accommodate our need for rest and relationships. By rest, I am not referring to leisure activities (that comes under play), but to relaxation, solitude and sleep. Without these, our lives and our relationships will disintegrate faster than we can repair them.

When I was a boy, my family conscientiously practiced the Sabbath. Not in the strict Jewish sense, but in principle. Our Sabbath began on Saturday afternoon when Mother did her baking for the week. The whole house took on the tantalizing aroma of baked goods — homemade bread, oatmeal cookies, chocolate cake and a variety of fruit pies. Once this was done, Mom began preparation for Sunday — she polished our good shoes, selected our clothes and made sure we had our baths before supper. After supper we sat around the kitchen table and studied our Sunday school lessons and memorized our verses. It was a quiet evening, a family affair, and it prepared our hearts for worship the next day.

Sunday mornings were special too, not like the quarrels which have become a pre-service ritual for so many families in the eighties. Our day started with a special breakfast — usually French toast and sausage, though sometimes we had Dad's favorite — biscuits and gravy. There were four of us kids, all under eleven at one time, but we still managed to make it to church on time. Mother always organized everything before going to bed Saturday night which significantly reduced the stress on Sunday morning. I can't remember any arguments about what to wear or whether we were going to church or not. Those things weren't even issues. Family tradition was established early, and carefully kept by all of us. That may sound restrictive, but it provided the routine which freed us to enjoy Sundays without a hassle.

Things changed as we got older. Mom and Dad still maintained their routine, but we boys began dating and coming in after the folks were in bed. On Sunday mornings, we slept in until the last minute and then rushed to get ready for church. Maybe some of that is inevitable, but something precious was lost in the transition.

Another tradition which I remember with fondness — Sunday dinners. This was a time for fellowship, and we almost never ate alone. It seemed that two or three families, sometimes more, always got together. After the meal we kids would disappear outdoors, and the adults would sit around the table for two or three hours, just talking. It seemed like such a waste to me then, just talking. Now, I know better. Few things in life are more important than deep sharing with good friends. It nourishes the soul, reaffirms one's place in the scheme of things. This too was part of our Sabbath ritual.

Twenty-one years in the pastoral ministry has convinced me that in order to be spiritually and emotionally whole, a sincere commitment to the Sabbath principle is absolutely manditory. Without it, we will never have the discipline required to establish and maintain an intimate relationship with God, a meaningful family life, nurturing friendships and a healthy sense of self. Relationships take time and planning, the kind of thing God had in mind when He gave us the Sabbath.

In Jewish tradition, the Sabbath wasn't just a day set apart from other days, but as S.R. Hirsch comments in *HOREB: A Philosophy of Jewish Laws and Observances,* "The Sabbath was not set apart to compartmentalize our lives, but so that your working days (might be) suffused with the spirit of the Sabbath."[3] In other words, every day should have something of the Sabbath in it — a time for rest, a time for relationships, and a time for worship.

It makes me think of something I read about Douglas Southall Freeman, busy editor of the Richmond, Virginia, *Times Dispatch.*

"He regularly arose at four o'clock each morning and would go straight to his office after having made a light breakfast. He would read, meditate, study, and reflect upon his writing assignments. He would rearrange the emphases of his life. He would think through the commitments of the day. Then he would enter into his regular appointment schedule at nine A.M. He usually would eat a light lunch in his office and then stay at his desk until two P.M. Then he would go home and redress for bed, and sleep two to three hours. Subsequently, he arose for the second time of the day, then read his stack of other newspapers while he awaited his dinner hour. He was then free to eat dinner with his wife and children and spend the forepart of the evening conversing with them. He went to bed around nine or ten P.M. Thus he had plenty of time for meditation, reflection, silence, and total quiet at times of day when everyone else was doing something else. In fact, he did everything, except that which he chose to do with others, at some other time than that which people ordinarily do it. As a result, he was able to get two days out of one and plenty of rest at the same time."[4]

I don't know if he called it the Sabbath principle or not, but that's what I have in mind when I say every day should have a bit of the Sabbath in it. Make sure you schedule time for rest, relationships, and worship. Wayne Oates writes in *Nurturing Silence in a Noisy Heart,* "I cannot tune time to your temperament for you. You should write down what your typical day's schedule tends to be like, and then begin landscaping the schedule to create some places and times of privacy for your regular cultivation of silence, communion with your inner being, and communion with the Eternal in your noisy heart."[5]

Since we live in a busy world, a noisy world, sometimes we have to take rest and quietness where we find it. I remember one hectic Wednesday some months ago when I did just that. Normally I go home shortly after noon on Wednesday so I can return for our evening service refreshed, but on this particular day a series of events had conspired to keep me at the church office.

Finally it was 5:30 p.m., and the last secretary was gone. For the first time since early morning, the office was quiet. I was whipped and wondering where I was going to get the energy to preach. I poured myself a cup of fresh coffee and walked back into my office where I was surprised by a breath of the Sabbath.

My office has a large window opening on an eleven-acre field. It was dusk and the last rays of the sun were glistening on the rain-wet grass. I watched as a man romped with two of the prettiest hunting dogs I'd ever seen. As I enjoyed the beauty of God's creation, man and beast, I felt the day's tension draining out of me. A quietness settled over me, and I sensed His presence. Joy swelled in my heart, and I was as fulfilled as I've ever been in my life. Don't ask me to explain it — I can't. I can only report what happened. For a minute, God met me in the midst of my busyness. Thankfully, I had sense enough to recognize Him and invite Him in.

That doesn't happen very often or it wouldn't be so special. Still, I think it happens more than we know. Many times we miss it, I'm afraid, because we haven't cultivated the Sabbath. Without the discipline of solitude, we have trouble recognizing it when it slips up on us.

Sunday is not a Sabbath for me and probably never will be as long as I am a pastor. I preach three Sunday morning services, frequently minister again that evening and then host a live 90-minute radio broadcast called "Straight from the Heart." Normally, I put in nearly twelve hours of very intense ministry and, believe me, that's work. However, for those who are not involved in full-time ministry, Sunday can be dedicated as a day of rest and worship.

I know of one young couple who has done just that. They both work outside the home and serve as volunteer assistants in the youth department at Christian Chapel. Recognizing the multiple demands being made upon them and their marriage, they made a covenant to keep Sundays for themselves. After worship, they share a private lunch and spend a quiet afternoon together. Sometimes they read or nap. If it's an especially nice day, they may picnic in the park or go for a walk. Whatever they choose to do, they do it together and without the distraction of others. It's not easy, but they recognize the value of it and have resisted all temptations to compromise. Needless to say, I applaud them.

How tragic that worship, which was designed for renewal and inspiration, has, for many believers, become nothing more than religious work — another responsibility in an already overdemanding world. Religion is now big business with multiple programs going seven days a week. If a church doesn't have a ministry designed to meet every need imaginable, it's considered archaic and unresponsive. Consequently, we are programmed for exhaustion. We are overcommitted, overextended and overworked. Rest and renewal have been replaced with busyness, and the church has become part of the problem it was designed to solve.

Gordon MacDonald shares an experience which illustrates what I mean. He says the most widely acclaimed Sunday in his five-year pastorate in New England occurred when a snowstorm forced the cancellation of Sunday services. Universally, the congregation recognized it as the most wonderful Lord's day they had ever had.

"I couldn't believe it," someone commented. "I had an entire twenty-four hours with my family; no schedule, nothing to do, just being quiet. It was marvelous." MacDonald adds, "(I couldn't help) wondering why we needed an 'act of God' to force us into doing what we all badly wanted to do: enjoy with those whom we love an interlude in the schedule away from all the routine busyness."[6]

We can blame the Church if we want, but some of the responsibility is ours too. And if the system is going to change, it will be from the inside out when persons just like you and me decide we've had enough. Will you accept the challenge? Will you make a commitment to observe the Sabbath in both your personal life and your church life? Frantic activity does not impress God, even when it's done in His name. He is more interested in what you are becoming than in what you are doing. You need to be involved in the ministry of your church, to be sure, but your involvement must be balanced with a commensurate commitment to your family and your inner world. Even Jesus Himself balanced His public ministry with solitude, time alone and with His friends, away from the press of the crowd.

As my ministry becomes more and more public, I find myself preaching conferences and conventions across the country. (Incidentally, I dislike the term "my ministry" because it is not really mine. It's God's, and I'm just a steward. But for the sake of conciseness I use it.) Often I will preach two or three times a day and minister individually between services. After a few days, I grow tired of the sound of my own voice. I long for privacy, for solitude, for silence. If I ignore that inner cry for renewal, it's not long until I am a hollow bundle of noise. If I still ignore it and plunge compulsively ahead, I lose my effectiveness and risk burning out.

In order to maintain my spiritual and emotional equilibrium, I must observe the Sabbath both weekly and daily. To achieve maximum benefit, I must rest the same day each week. Sometimes this is not possible, but when it's not, I almost always pay for it. After experimenting with several days, Brenda and I have settled on Monday for our Sabbath. There's nothing special about Monday, but after Sunday's exhausting schedule I need a day to recover. Besides, there seems to be less scheduled early in the week, making it easier to honor our commitment.

Frequently, we stay in all day, enjoying our privacy and our home. If we do venture out, it is usually just to share a quiet lunch in a nearby restaurant. Brenda and I use Monday to catch up on our rest, and we often nap for two hours or more in the afternoon. We talk at length, sharing deeply, catching up on the things we've been too busy to share with each other during the week. We read, listen to music, or even watch an old movie on the VCR.

Leah becomes part of the Sabbath when she comes in from school around three o'clock. We play board games on the floor in front of the fireplace and talk, especially around the dinner table. Deliberately we relive our family history, each one of us sharing a favorite memory, enjoying the experience again. If one of us has a pressing concern that can't wait, we deal with that, too. However, for the most part, Mondays are reserved for renewing our relationships. Problems can be dealt with on another day.

We don't really forget about the world, but we do keep it at arm's distance. A page from my journal will give you an idea of what I mean:

"It's bitterly cold outside and everything is iced with a thin frosting of snow. Inside, the room is warm, music is playing and Brenda and Leah are in the kitchen making blueberry muffins. Love permeates everything — God's love, our love.

"God, don't let me forget the cold and the hungry — those who aren't feeling loved. All of them — the winos huddled in doorways seeking shelter from the cutting wind; the unemployed sleeping in their cars, hoping for a brighter tomorrow; even the wealthy who are cold on the inside because they are loveless.

"Make me sensitive and compassionate. Let me see the hurt, hear the cries that are never uttered. Let me give love. Let me extend a helping hand, let me share an affirming word, let me be hospitable.

"God, I'm doing what I can — help me to do more. Help me to reach out farther.

"How do you feed a hungry world? One person at a time!

"How do you love a lonely world? One person at a time!

"I'll do my best, Lord. I really will."

Without the Sabbath, without rest and renewal, without the love of family, I would never have the resources to reach out to a hurting world. Rather than isolating us, the Sabbath renews us so that we can effectively involve ourselves in a broken world.

Footnotes

1. Alan D. Goldberg, "The Sabbath: Implications for Mental Health," *Counseling and Values,* 31, No. 2, (Apr. 1987), pp. 148,149.

2. Ibid., p. 149.

3. S. R. Hirsch, HOREB: *A Philosophy of Jewish Laws and Observances* (New York: Soncino Press, 1962).

4. Wayne E. Oates, *Nurturing Silence In a Noisy Heart* (Garden City: Doubleday & Company, Inc., 1979), p. 32.

5. Ibid., p. 33.

6. Gordon MacDonald, *Restoring Your Spiritual Passion* (Nashville: Oliver Nelson, A Division of Thomas Nelson Publishers, 1986), pp. 24,25.

Chapter 6

MAKING REST WORK

"It happened again, Lord.
I got up late . . . tired . . . running behind.
I had an early appointment — then a hundred
pressing details.

"Others waiting on me to complete my work
    so they can get at theirs.
    More counseling,
        phone calls to return,
            people to see . . .
                things to do.

"Here it is, 6 P.M.,
and I'm finally getting
to my morning devotion!

"Forgive me, Father,
You deserve better . . . I need more.
Make me sensitive to the demands of my body.
Teach me to live within my limits,
    physically and spiritually.

"Today's problems started two nights ago.
I stayed up too late,
    and again, last night.

"If I'm going to work as hard as I do,
    make this many demands on my body,
        then I'm going to have to listen
            when it screams for rest!

"Teach me to listen, Lord,
    to You and to my body."

Does that sound familiar? Probably. After all, busyness is a way of life in the eighties and has been for most of us since we were just children in elementary school. It starts with music lessons, Little League, Girl Scouts, church camp and a host of other legitimate activities. By the time we reach high school, we are addicted. Year Book, drama, jazz choir and the French Club all compete for our time. Then there's the youth group, Friday night football games, dates, and a part-time job. Not to mention homework and family time.

It's even worse in college. By the time we graduate, frantic activity and the accompanying tiredness have become an accepted way of life. In fact, it seems to be a measure of our commitment, our importance. Yet for all of that, we have a vague feeling that we're missing something, so we redouble our efforts, increase our involvements and reduce our joy yet again. We find ourselves doing more and more, yet enjoying it less.

We complain frequently about how busy we are, about being too involved, about always being tired, but we never do anything about it. Sometimes we pause in our mad rush through life to wistfully dream about a restful evening at home. Yet when, by some stroke of fate, we find ourselves alone for the evening, we're wound so tight we can't even enjoy it.

Tilden Edwards describes it this way:

"It is late evening. We are alone, perhaps for the first time since we woke. Bits and pieces from the day dart in and out of our consciousness. Little desires and fears for tomorrow scatter us further. The more that rushes through our minds, the more complicated and anxious life seems. Maybe TV will help settle us down — or the newspaper — or some work — or sex or a big snack. Less seems to gnaw at us then. Life stays put for a moment. We feel in control again — we're 'doing' something — anything.

"The aftereffect of the doing leaves us less anxious, but more drugged. We've exchanged a gnawing anxiety for a dulled sensibility . . . You and I share such a (life). It is usually bearable; it even seems 'normal,' out of sheer habit. Sometimes it is even fun. But it is not fulfilling."[1]

And I might add, it's not the Abundant Life Jesus promised!

Most of our work is not that physically demanding, and yet we often drag home hardly able to put one foot in front of the other. Compare our exhaustion with the satisfied tiredness our grandparents felt at the end of their day. They were tired too, but it was from the outside-in. Ours, I think, is just the opposite. We're tired from the inside-out. Our weariness is more emotional than physical. Our spirits are depleted. The constant pressure, the continual interaction with people, taxes our emotional energies. Add a touch of interpersonal conflict, and the drain increases dramatically.

A good night's sleep helps, but it cannot restore our spiritual and emotional energies unless it is supplemented by the inner disciplines of renewal — silence, solitude, inwardness. Add to these the renewal generated by special friends, and you have a lifestyle which is continually replenishing the inner man.

It sounds easy, but it's not. Ours is a noisy world. Even as I type these words, I hear the sound of an airplane on its final approach to the airport, traffic in the streets, a lawn mower. Consider the outrageous number of TV's, stereos and radios all adding to the din. Our addiction to noise is almost absolute. Parks and beaches resound to the blaring of portable radios. Joggers can't make it an hour without noise, so they run to the beat of their headsets. Now add to this the almost constant clamor of conversation, and you can see why it's so hard to incorporate silence into our frantic lives.

"Silence is not native to my world," writes Wayne Oates in *Nurturing Silence In a Noisy Heart.* "Silence, more than likely, is a stranger to your world, too. If you and I ever have silence in our noisy hearts, we are going to have to grow it."[2] So how do we go about cultivating silence in a busy world beset with noise? First, we have to take time for it, carve out a space in our crowded lives. Remember, the noise we hear is inner as well as outer. Noisy thoughts clamor for our attention. Budgets, programs, and other details from our workaday world intrude upon the silence within. Even as we dedicate a physical time and place for silence, so we must cast out the noisy intruders who would turn our inner sanctuary into a maelstrom of emotion.

I've always been something of a solitary person; although, I do have a deep need for friends. Consequently, silence may come a bit more natural to me than most. As a boy, I always seemed to have a private place, a hideaway where I could go and be alone. Once it was a tool shed attached to the garage. I personalized it by turning a large storage shelf into a bunk, moving in Mom's old radio and displaying all of my fishing gear. Almost every day, I spent time there, alone with the silence and my thoughts.

Another private place was my Grandma Miller's house. Grandad died when I was nine. After that, I began spending four and five nights a week with her. She couldn't read or write and didn't trust electricity. It was like stepping back into another age. Many a night we sat in comfortable silence, each entertained by our own thoughts, wrapped in the soft glow of a kerosene lamp. Sometimes we talked, but it wasn't necessary. Silence was a friend we both knew well and welcomed.

The outdoors became yet another sanctuary of silence in my young life. As a boy, I tramped the river bottoms in northeastern

Colorado both summer and winter. I fished and hunted, sometimes with friends, but more often alone. Early on, I made friends with myself and learned to enjoy my own company. That's not to say I was self-centered as much as I was self-reliant. Others were not the source of my happiness, nor was I dependent on their approval for my self-image. Only now, these many years later, am I able to appreciate how liberating that was and is.

If silence hasn't been a regular part of your world, this may seem a little unusual, perhaps even frightening. Susan Annette Muto says, "A common problem, related to why we may seek to escape silence, is the discovery that it evokes nameless misgivings, guilt feelings, strange, disquieting anxiety. Anything is better than this mess, and so we flick on the radio or pick up the phone and talk to a friend. *If we can pass through these initial fears and remain silent, we may experience a gradual waning of inner chaos.* Silence becomes like a creative space in which we regain perspective on the whole."[3] In disciplined silence, we forget our problems for a while and remember who we are.

Finding time for silence and solitude is a constant challenge even when you believe in it and value it highly. The world is constantly encroaching — an important meeting, your daughter's spring concert, special services at church, a new project. The list is endless. Again and again, I have fallen prey to the press of busyness. Soon my life is devoid of silence, then joy. Finally life's meaningfulness is lost as well. At those times I'm not only tired, but often depressed as well. Usually I can't put my finger on what's really wrong, but life is flat and tasteless. Now and then, I have a vague sense that something is missing, but I can't quite get a handle on it.

When I've had all I can take, my body usually lets me know. I get a severe headache. The kind that makes it impossible to work or socialize. Out of necessity, I shut out the world for a few hours, sometimes even overnight. Then it comes back to me. I haven't been practicing the rhythm of life. I haven't made time for myself, time for solitude. Even in the midst of that realization, I am severely tempted to turn on the radio or pick up the phone and call someone. Silence has become a stranger, and I can hardly bring myself to seek it out.

Why do I tell you that? Because I want you to know that I struggle with the same pressures that you do. And I fail more often than I would like to admit. Still I keep going back. In the midst of my frantic faithfulness, I hear God say, " 'Be still, and know that I am God . . .' " (Ps. 46:10).

Sometimes I need help finding my way. Busyness has so desensitized me that I can't feel. I'm numb. With determined deliberateness, I do the things that have worked in the past. I brew a cup of coffee. I light the kerosene lamp in my study. I force myself to sit and be quiet. At first, half-a-hundred thoughts wrestle for my attention. Phone calls I need to make. Things I need to do tomorrow, chores I should be doing around the house right now. His words again, "Be still . . . be still . . . ." Bit by bit I feel the tensions slip away. The noise of the world is pushed back for a little while. Even the discordant voices within grow quiet.

Out of the stillness comes a picture from the past, indistinct at first, just a dim outline. Then I give myself to it. I embrace it, and it all comes rushing back — the colors, the smells, the sounds.

Even as I write this, I embrace such a memory. It's as real as the day it happened, maybe more so. It was a Saturday afternoon in early spring. We were living in Houston where I was associate pastor at a troubled church. For weeks I had been under tremendous pressure to resign, but I stubbornly resisted. Not the least of my reasons was the fact that Brenda's mother had, had a cancerous tumor removed and was undergoing radiation treatment. The last thing Brenda needed was the additional stress of moving, not to mention the very real possibility that the move would be out of the state.

Suddenly the setting sun broke through the dark clouds of a retreating thunderstorm, giving the rain-washed neighborhood a just-bathed freshness. For a moment, I was transfixed. I forgot my half-finished sermon notes, Brenda's mother's illness, the church troubles . . . everything. I could hear Brenda in the kitchen preparing supper, and I felt a deep contentment.

After a few minutes I wrote:

"I sit here
in the near darkness
of a late, rain-washed afternoon.
Thunder growls deeply in the distance,
drowning out the sound
of the softly falling rain.

"Yellow light from the kitchen
spills into my mostly dark study,
and I can hear you banging pans
and humming softly.

"I feel contented,
but I can remember
when it wasn't so.
When my life was
mostly sadness and shadows,
before the yellow light
of your love came spilling in.

"Now my life is
mostly sunshine,
and what sadness remains
huddles in the darkest corners unacknowledged,
unless you are unhappy
or away."

Even now, that memory has the power to refresh me. I let it carry me back. I live it again, feel the feelings, and as I do, I sense the tension leaving me. Unfortunately, such an experience is rare indeed for many people. For them, memories are random at best, or reserved for family reunions or a wake. How tragic, for when we ignore our memories or relegate them to special occasions, we rob ourselves of their renewing power.

This practice is not original with me. It's a biblical concept. Again and again God commands His people to establish memorials as reminders of His great faithfulness. Holy communion is probably the best known to the church, but there are many others. One of my favorites comes from Joshua 4:1-3,6,7:

"When the whole nation had finished crossing the Jordan, the Lord said to Joshua, 'Choose twelve men from among the people, one from each tribe, and tell them to take up twelve stones from the middle of the Jordan from right where the priests stood and to carry them over with you and put them down at the place where you stay tonight . . . to serve as a sign among you. In the future, when your children ask you, "What do these stones mean?" tell them that the flow of the Jordan was cut off before the ark of the covenant of the Lord. When it crossed the Jordan, the waters of the Jordan were cut off. These stones are to be a memorial to the people of Israel forever.' "

Read the Psalms and see how often the writers recall how God brought them out of Egypt, how He divided the Red Sea so they could cross on dry ground, how He quenched their thirst with water from a rock and how He fed them with fresh manna every morning. When the present seemed hopeless, they reached back and were encouraged as they relived past victories and re-experienced His faithfulness.

Arthur Gordon writes, "Not long ago I came to one of those bleak periods that many of us encounter from time to time, a sudden drastic dip in the graph of living when everything goes stale and flat, energy wanes, enthusiasm dies. Every morning I would clench my teeth and mutter: 'Today life will take on some of its old meaning.' . . . But the barren days went by and the paralysis grew worse . . . ."[4]

In desperation he went to see a doctor, not a psychiatrist, just a gruff old doctor. Beneath his surface gruffness though, there lay great wisdom and compassion. He told Gordon to drive to the beach alone the following morning, arriving not later than nine o'clock. He could take some lunch, but he was not to read, write, listen to the radio, or talk to anyone. Then, almost as an after-thought, the doctor scrawled some instructions on a pad of prescription blanks and handed them to him. "Take them one at a time," he said, "at three-hour intervals."

The next morning Gordon did as he was instructed. The beach was deserted, lonely, a northeaster was blowing; the sea looked gray and angry. For a while, he sat in the car, moodily, the whole day stretching emptily before him. Finally he took out the folded prescription blanks and opened the first one. On it the doctor had written: "Listen carefully."

His first reaction was amazement. The doctor had ruled out music, newscasts and human conversation. What else was there? Still, he gave it a try. At first all he heard was the screech of a gull, the steady roar of the sea, the whine of the wind. It seemed so pointless, and he was tempted with anger. In desperation he persisted and after a while, he realized his mind was slowing down, coming to a rest. When you truly listen for something outside yourself, he concluded, you have to silence the clamorous voices within. Sitting there, he found himself thinking of things bigger than himself and that was a welcome relief.

The second prescription said: "Try reaching back." For Gordon, this was the most pleasant part of the treatment. He left the car and started tramping along the dunes. He found a sheltered place and lay down on the sun-warmed sand. Lying there, he wondered if perhaps the doctor had sent him to the beach because it was a place of happy memories. Maybe that's what he was supposed to reach for — the wealth of happiness that lies half-forgotten in the past.

As he peered into the past, the recollections that came to mind were happy but indistinct. He decided to experiment, to work on those vague impressions as a painter would, retouching the colors, strengthening the outlines. He chose specific incidents and recaptured as many details as possible. He visualized people complete with dress and gestures. He listened carefully for the exact sound of their voices, the echo of their laughter. Soon his depression began to give way to the happiness of the past.

The third prescription instructed him to examine his motives, and the fourth simply said, "Write your worries in the sand." By the day's end, the paralysis of depression was broken and he was well on his way to recovering his zest for living. A simple, but effective cure. Yet, as I think about it and compare it to my life's experience, I see it as more than a cure. It's preventative medicine — more a way of warding off depression rather than treating it, especially the part about reaching back. Happy, positive memories have the power to infuse the more difficult present with a sense of hope.[5]

It works for me when I take the time to do it, and the more consistent I am, the more faithful I am to make a quiet space in every day, the better it works. Soon the laughter and love of the past warm even the most disappointing day. I'm not talking about denying the reality of the present, only putting it into perspective. Try reaching back, try making memories a part of your daily rest, and see if your attitude doesn't improve.

Life, as you well know, is a constant mixture of success and failure, joy and sorrow, hope and despair. It is our responsibility to sift through these experiences, choosing which ones to remember and which ones to forget. Happy people, for the most part, have mastered the holy art of remembering good things. When the present is painful or foreboding, they reach back and get some happiness from the past.

Over the years I've become more consistent and, as I have, my appreciation for rest and for memories has grown. Some months ago I wrote in my journal:

"Lord,
thank You for the gift of memory.

With it I can leave
the suffocating confines of an overcrowded schedule
and return, for a few minutes,
to the barefoot days of my youth.

"I feel sun-warmed sand between my toes.
I sit, half-hypnotized,
watching the slow-moving South Platte.
The smell of wood smoke blends
with the fragrance of fresh-cut alfalfa.
It only lasts for a couple of minutes,
but for that brief time,
I'm a boy again —
    carefree,
    roaming the river bottom,
        living my own version of Huck Finn.

"Thank You, Lord, for the gift of memory.
With it I can put
present pressures into perspective.
With determined deliberateness,
I recall other times when trouble
threatened to overwhelm me.
A Christmas in Holly
when we were flat broke,
and feeling blue.
Then on Christmas Eve,
You came through — a check for $224!
Oh, what a Christmas that was!

"The numbers are bigger now,
but the pressures are the same,
and so are You.

"Thank You, Lord, for the gift of memory.
Past joys enrich my busy days.
Mini-vacations,
    trips to the past,
        return me to my present tasks renewed.

> Past victories put today's challenges
> into proper perspective.

"I remember, and I'm a better man.
I remember, and I'm blessed.

" 'I remember the days of old;
I meditate on all thy works . . . .' " (Ps. 143:5 *King James Version*).

Special friends are important too, another element of rest. Someone to be with when you have to get away, but can't bear to be by yourself. They provide a safe place in a demanding world, a place where you can let your hair down and be yourself, a place where you don't have to weigh every word. Persons with whom, as Emerson said, "I may think outloud." With them, you can share your dreams without fear of being put down. You can share your visions without being misunderstood and even share your fears without risk to the relationship.

Tilden Edwards says, "Such a spiritual friend can be enormously supportive to us, and we to them . . . When someone else knows and cares, then we pay that much more attention to what we're doing."[6] M. Basil Pennington in "A Place Apart," writes, " . . . anyone who has been graced with true friendship knows the cost and knows the worth."[7]

I have been blessed with and I know the worth of special friends. Many is the time I have been at my wit's end — not really discouraged but just undone by a needy world. A couple of hours with such a friend can restore my energies and rekindle my passion. There are times when we need to be totally alone in order to rest, to be sure, but there are other times when only a friend can renew our vision. I agree with Michael Benson who prayed, "Lord, You know I am not particularly heroic or saintly; that I need someone who will be my friend on this spiritual journey. Let them find me through my willingness to be a spiritual friend. Amen."[8]

Special books are also part of the rhythm of rest in my life — not necessarily heavy books or books that tax my mind, but sensitive books which touch my soul. Books which give me a glimpse of life in both its tenderness and its tragedy. Books which put me in touch with my own life experiences. As far as I'm concerned, such a book is worth anything it costs and more.

In one of Benet's radio dramas, a maidservant cries, "Life is not lost by dying. Life is lost minute by minute, day by dragging day, in all our thousand small uncaring ways."[9] And so it is, at least in my life. Many are the times I've been numb, just going through the motions, sleepwalking as it were, when a special book touched me, and I began to live again, feel again.

About ten or eleven years ago, when my daughter was about six years old, I had such an experience. It happened while reading a meditation called "Gift from a Hair Dryer" written by Mary Jean Irion and included in her book, *Yes, World: A Mosaic of Meditation*. I share it with you now in hopes that you too might be moved as deeply as I was.

"As she scrambles out of the Saturday night bath and shampoo, dripping dark green footprints on the light green mat, you throw a towel around her head and rub vigorously as she jumps up and down.

" 'Mommy, I've got goose pimples!'

" 'Stand still,' you say, handing her another towel. 'Dry yourself while I rub your hair.'

"Five minutes later she is pink pajamaed, clean-toothed and sitting crosslegged on her bed, damp hair going in all directions. She resembles nothing so much as a newly-hatched chicken. You perch beside her and plug in the hand-operated hair dryer, pointing it at the nape of her neck. 'It's nice and warm,' she says, reaching for a book. 'I'll read you a story while it dries.'

" 'Good,' you say, combing from south to north on the back of her head and directing the warm air stream into the moving hair, watching it fall in layers, finely, as it sifts apart from the damp mass. A horizontal part moves upward following the comb. Over and over again — south to north, hair falling, air blowing.

" ' "John and Cindy had a little dog. He was brown and white. His name was Toby." ' Second-grade reading books are fascinating to second graders, and that is as it should be. You find your fascination elsewhere, in the way the light falls on the gold-brown strands.

" ' "Go get the ball, Toby," ' she reads on. You are trying to decide whether she is really quite beautiful or just ordinary and beloved. Likely not beautiful. But beloved.

"The comb lifts the hair, baring a pink ear scrubbed to Saturday night perfection. Something about the pink ear takes you back over the years, and you remember this same head, baby-bald as a darning egg. Then came blonde curls. Now no curls and not any special color, but clean and soft and shining, warm-laid on the side of her cheek.

" ' "John and Cindy went looking for their dog." ' You are not listening.

"Comb and dry, comb and dry. You half close your eyes and pick another memory out of her blowing hair. She was three that summer on Cape Cod when the strong sea wind blew the curls up from her neck just like this. You remember how she turned around and suddenly up went the bangs, baring a white forehead above sun-pink nose and cheeks. You remember the unbelievable quantity of sand she carried home on her scalp that day to be brushed out on the cottage floor. How little she was then! And now seven. Seven!

"The air current swings her hair suddenly to one side, and she is five again, skipping off to her first day at kindergarten, the breezes undoing all the work of a careful comb as they play through her hair, swaying it like this in rhythm to her skipping. The cadence of her merry gait captures you completely even now, two years later.

"She coughs you back into Saturday night on the edge of her bed and goes on reading. ' "The children asked the grocery store man if he had seen Toby." '

" 'Turn around now,' you say. 'Let's do the other side. It's dry over here.' Yes, she is beautiful. You have decided it, and that is that.

"Comb and dry, comb and dry. 'Soon I won't be able to do this any more,' you say to yourself, knowing that the little straight bob must inevitably yield to grown-up coiffures and ugly curlers. What will she be like at fourteen? Where will her hair be blowing then? And sixteen and eighteen — you suppose boys will love to watch her hair blow as you do now. And some of them will feel it on their faces, and one of them will marry her, and her hair will be perfect under the veil, and there will be her hair spread out on his pillow . . . oh, you hate him a little and wonder where he is at this moment and whether he'll be good to her . . . they will grow old together . . . the gold-brown hair will be gray, and you will be gone, and then she will be gone . . . this very hair that now your fingers smooth . . .

"All the tears of the world swim for a second in your eyes as you snatch the plug out of the socket suddenly and gather her into your arms burying your face in the warm hair as if you could somehow seal this moment against all time.

" 'Hey, don't you know we're just at the end of the story?' she asks, surprised by your embrace.

" 'Yes, honey. Of course.'

" 'I peeked ahead. They find their dog. It's a happy story.'

" 'I knew it would be.'

"She reads the last page. You sing an evening song together, exchange kisses on each other's noses, turn out the light and go downstairs to finish the ironing as if nothing bittersweet and wonderful had happened."[10]

The only thing better than reading that is living it, and yet her words stop me in my tracks. How many times have I lived moments like that without realizing it? Now tears are swimming in my eyes. I put my finger between the pages and pray. First I seek forgiveness for all the times I've missed life's special moments. Then I thank God for Leah and all the moments we've had. Finally I vow again to slow down, to enjoy life, to live it to the fullest.

In the Talmud, the collected wisdom of the rabbis of the first five centuries, it is written, "In the world to come, each of us will be called to account for all the good things God put on earth which we refused to enjoy."[11]

The first time I read Irion's poignant account, I was so deeply touched that I got up and went to the door of Leah's room and watched in wistful silence as she played Barbies. My heart swelled with love and thanksgiving, and I realized that this was Abundant Life, not all there was to it, but definitely Abundant Life. She sensed my presence and glanced a question in my direction. I smiled and spread my arms wide, "I just wanted to say I love you big — this much!"

With experiences like that, life can't grow old. It's renewed day by day. The rhythm of rest — silence, solitude, memory, mini-vacations, special friends, books that touch the heart, and deep sleep. Taken together, day by day they renew us, cause us to ". . . mount up with wings as eagles; . . . run, and not be weary; . . . walk, and not faint" (Is. 40:31 *King James Version*).

Footnotes

1. Tilden H. Edwards, "Living Simply Through the Day," *Disciplines For The Inner Life* by Bob Benson and Michael W. Benson (Waco: Word Books, 1985), pp. 13,14.

2. Oates, p. 3.

3. Susan A. Muto, *Pathways Of Spiritual Living* (Garden City: Doubleday & Company, Inc., 1984).

4. Gordon, p. 83.

5. Ibid. (paraphrased)

6. Edwards, p. 104.

7. M. Basil Pennington, "A Place Apart," quoted in *Disciplines For The Inner Life,* p. 104.

8. Bob Benson and Michael W. Benson, *Disciplines For The Inner Life,* p. 103.

9. Frederick B. Speakman, *The Salty Tang* (Westwood: Fleming H. Revell Company), p. 128.

10. Mary Jean Irion, "Gift From A Hair Dryer," (originally from *United Church Herald,* Nov. 1962) *Yes, World: A Mosaic of Meditation* (Richard W. Baron Publishing Company, Inc., 1970).

11. Kushner, p. 57.

Part III

WORSHIP

Part III

WORSHIP

Worship is the spontaneous, irrepressible cry of the heart when the glory of the Creator breaks in upon it. Sometimes it happens in a sanctuary or synagogue. It did in the case of Simeon when he took the baby Jesus in his arms and praised God, saying: " 'Sovereign Lord, as you have promised, you now dismiss your servant in peace. For my eyes have seen your salvation . . .' " (Luke 2:29,30). That was his way of saying that he had seen it all! That there was nothing left to live for. For this moment, he was born and had lived, and now his life's purpose was fulfilled.

Sometimes it happens when we are under pressure, facing circumstances which are beyond us. That's how it was for Jacob. He spent the whole night, alone, wrestling in the dark, on the muddy river bank with a man who was more than just a man. Afterwards, he could only talk about it in hushed tones and then only to say, " '. . . I saw God face to face, and yet my life was spared' " (Gen. 32:30). That's the essence of worship, isn't it? " '. . . I saw God face to face . . .' "

It happens, I think, more often than most of us realize. Usually we only see it in retrospect, and then we are undone. How could

I have been so blind? How could I have been so dumb? Then we feel unworthy, sinful — like Peter who fell to his knees and cried, " 'Go away from me, Lord; I am a sinful man!' " (Luke 5:8). But He doesn't go away. He stays with us, and we begin to see all of life through different eyes. That, too, is worship.

Once we begin to understand something of the mystery of His presence, all of life becomes a sanctuary and each experience, no matter how mundane, an opportunity to worship. The beauty of nature causes us to exclaim, "Good job, God! Good job!" The birth of a child, the majesty of a great piece of music, a wedding, a special book or movie, even the death of a friend or family member all become an invitation to experience His presence, an opportunity to worship.

This section is not so much a treatise on worship as it is an invitation to share in the actual experience. It's not even a call to worship, at least not in a traditional sense. Still, if it goes the way I hope it does, you will hear His Spirit calling to yours or as the Scriptures say, "Deep calls to deep . . . ." (Ps. 42:7).

Hugh Prather, writing in *I Touch The Earth, The Earth Touches Me*, puts it like this: "I associate this spiritual way of seeing with many causes: with music and poetry, with sunsets and seas, with friends who are friends, with love, and now and then with a book or a passage within a book. These things have at times inspired me to this broader vision, but rarely have I been able to return and use one of them to recapture it. If I try, the poem or song will have lost its magic, and I only receive an echo of my previous wonder."[1]

It's like that for me, too. If I don't stop and enjoy it to the fullest when it first moves me, I will miss it. When I come back to it, it's never the same. If it happens for you while reading this section, put your finger between the pages, forget the book for a bit and let your spirit soar to meet His. The book will still be there when you're finished. But if you fail to take advantage of your moment of inspiration, it's lost, gone forever. It will never happen quite like that again.

Footnotes

1. Hugh Prather, *I Touch The Earth, The Earth Touches Me* (Garden City: Doubleday & Company, Inc., 1972).

Chapter 7

TOUCHING THE ETERNAL

"Recent archaeological discoveries uncovered letters written by martyrs during the first three centuries following Christ. Just before death, one saint penned, 'In a dark hole I have found cheerfulness; in a place of bitterness and death I have found rest. While others weep I have found laughter, where others fear I have found strength. Who would believe that in a state of misery I have had great pleasure; that in a lonely corner I have had glorious company, and in the hardest bonds perfect repose. All those things Jesus has granted me. He is with me, comforts me and fills me with joy. He drives bitterness from me and fills me with strength and consolation.' "[1]

How is it that a prisoner, facing death for his faith, living out his days in a dark hole, can know joy and contentment like that, while a successful person, enjoying all the amenities of the good life is miserable and depressed? Don't settle for the easy answers — "Money can't buy happiness." Or, "If you don't have a good marriage and family, nothing else matters . . ." That's all well and good, but those aren't the only kind of people who have a mediocre existence.

What about those Christians who are faithful, who have godly families, who are successful in business, yet know little or nothing of real contentment, not to mention the Abundant Life. Those, who in their heart of hearts, live with a secret disappointment. They wouldn't admit it to anyone, maybe not even to themselves, but life hasn't been all they expected. Marriage, children, career success, and even Christianity have all failed to produce the promised return. What about them?

Jesus said that He came to bring us abundant life (John 10:10), yet most of the Christians I know are living on the ragged edge. Oh, they have their moments but, for the most part, it's hard to distinguish the quality of their lives from that of the unregenerate. Why? Is abundant life an empty promise? An unrealistic expectation in our stressful culture?

The Abundant Life, I believe, is foreign to many believers because we are largely ignorant of its dynamics. Mistakenly, we assume it is something which happens independent of our efforts. Not so. It originates with God, to be sure, and without His direct intervention in our lives we will never have it. Yet what He gives us is the capacity for abundant life rather than the reality of it.

It is both a gift and a discipline. It's the quality of life imparted to the individual when he accepts Jesus Christ as his personal Lord and Savior. Without the "gift of abundant life," there is nothing a person can do to create it. A right attitude and positive thinking can improve the quality of anyone's life, but it will not be "abundant life" in the scriptural sense.

Every believer possesses the gift, that God-given potential to experience life to the very fullest. Yet without the disciplines, it is nothing more than an unrealized possibility and there is no burden more difficult to bear. To live with the knowledge of what might have been, what should have been, is torment indeed. "Would we were like animals," mused the poet, Walt Whitman, observing the difficulties of man, knowing human frustrations, and noticing the tranquility of animals, "for I have not seen animals weep in the night because of the guilt of their sins. I have not seen them pour out their lives in remorse."[2] Such is often the fate of those who have the gift, the potential, yet lack the reality of abundant life.

The spiritual disciplines which transform this possibility into a reality are detailed and well documented. They are relatively simple, but they are not easy. They include, but are not limited to: daily prayer, the study of the Scriptures, regular fasting, meditation, solitude and corporate worship. Conscientious practitioners, since the time of Christ, have experienced the Abundant Life as the result of these disciplines, and we can too.

Another equally important, but less recognized discipline is the rhythm of life — that delicate balance between work and rest, worship and play. Meaningful work gives our lives definition and purpose. Yet, without a corresponding amount of rest, even creative or spiritual work becomes tedious. Work without rest inevitably produces burnout. Worship and play must then be added to the work/rest cycle to produce the Abundant Life.

Rest restores our physical vitality and renews our emotional energies. In restful solitude, we forget the world with its pressing demands for a while and remember who we are. Worship goes a step farther and enables us to forget ourselves for a while and remember Who God is. It puts everything into perspective. In worship we remember the goodness and the greatness of God. Against this backdrop, life's most disconcerting difficulties become somehow manageable. Or as the apostle said, ". . . If God is for us, who can be against us?" (Rom. 8:31).

The final element in the rhythm of life is play. It relieves the tension and gives balance to the whole of life. By divine design, we need it all and we ignore this rhythm at our own peril. Without it, the hardiest among us risk burnout. Life's richness hangs by a slender thread. With these thoughts in mind, let's turn our attention to worship.

First, worship enables us to forget ourselves for a while. It's the only cure for our deadly self-centeredness. Almost nothing in life is more debilitating. The more we focus on our needs, our desires and our rights, the more unhappy we become. You may be ambitious, brilliant, successful and even powerful without being other-centered, but you will never be happy. That's a fact of life as inexorable as death.

For all of its laughter and surface gaiety, our world is not a very happy place. That really shouldn't surprise us. I mean, how can we expect to be happy when we violate almost every principle of the Abundant Life? We work too long, play too fast, laugh too loud and worship too little. We are hedonistic, always looking out for number one. We are materialistic. We buy things we don't need and can't afford in order to impress people we don't even like. Like a bunch of pack rats, we are constantly carrying home the latest gadget in a misdirected effort to satisfy our gnawing emptiness. Our only hope is to learn to love God and people instead of things.

Our self-centeredness manifests itself even in our worship. Listen to the language we use, the questions we ask each other. "What did you get out of that service?" "There's really nothing at that church for me." "I'm not being fed." I could continue, but surely you get the point. The disproportionate ways we invest the church's limited resources in favor of the local congregation is only more evidence of our ingrained selfishness. Where is our social concern? Where is our world vision?

No wonder we are unfulfilled. People who live only for themselves soon become obnoxious to themselves. Noted psychologist, William James, was often heard to say, "The only truly happy people I know are those who have found a cause greater than themselves to live for."

Worship is our only hope. But for worship to work, it will have to be real instead of religious, and that's not easy for those of us who are so indoctrinated in duplicity. John Killinger put his finger on it when he said, "The self we send out to meet God is almost always a false self."[3]

Pause for a moment and be totally honest. Are you natural, are you really yourself when you approach God or do you find yourself reverting to your religious conditioning? Are your prayers conversational or pious? Formal or friendly?

How we worship depends an awfully lot on how we perceive God and what He expects from us. If we see Him other than He really is, then we may spend our entire lives in an elaborate masquerade. Unfortunately, most of us have been taught to say right things rather than real things, to present our religious self rather than our real self to God.

Nowhere is this tragic truth more clearly seen than in the Old Testament story of Abraham and Sarah. God visited Abraham one day and told him that his wife Sarah was going to bear him a son about the same time the next year. Now Sarah was standing just inside the tent door, listening. That announcement struck her as rather humorous and well it might have. Abraham was nearly one hundred years of age. She was doubly cursed herself — barren and well past the age of childbearing or in the words of the King James text, ". . . it ceased to be with Sarah after the manner of women" (Gen. 18:11). To top it all off, she was probably over ninety herself.

Sarah's mistake wasn't in laughing. Anyone in their right mind would have laughed, given those circumstances. She laughed because if she didn't laugh, she would cry. What she had just overheard was too good to be true. I think God Himself would have shared in her laughter if she would have given Him half a chance, but she didn't. As soon as she realized that God was on to her, she froze up. Genesis 18:15 says, "Sarah was afraid, so she lied and said, 'I did not laugh.'"

What happened? For just a moment she forgot herself and simply responded honestly, naturally, from the heart. But as soon as she realized what she was doing, she became self-conscious and reverted to her religious conditioning. The God she knew was humorless, the image of God that she had wouldn't allow her to be herself. As a consequence, she ended up lying and sending out a "false self" to be with God. What could have been a glorious worship experience turned into a cheap masquerade.

For worship to be real, for it to be effective, both for God and for ourselves, we must be transparent and uninhibited. "There is a tradition in both Judaism and Christianity of the 'holy fool,' the simple, uneducated, unsophisticated person who serves God spontaneously and enthusiastically, without stopping to think about what he is doing. His serving is especially beloved because no intellectual barriers come between him and his God. One of the most beloved stories of medieval Christianity is the story of the Lady's Juggler. Every one of the faithful was coming to bring his or her gift to honor the Virgin on her holiday. They were fine, expensive gifts, handwoven tapestries, jewel-encrusted crowns. One poor, simple young man had no present to bring and no money with which to buy one. But he could juggle. So he danced and juggled before the statue of the Virgin, to the horror of all the very proper spectators, and because his juggling was from the heart, it was the most acceptable gift of all."[4]

Now that's what I'm talking about. When a person truly worships, he forgets himself and what others might think of him. God becomes everything. "A Roman Catholic scholar, Romano Guardini, has said in his book, *The Spirit of the Liturgy,* that man, when he is most truly worshipping God, is playing."[5] John Killinger adds, "I find that a singularly attractive idea. It is a real test for the liturgy of the church: does the liturgy really make it more easy, or more difficult, for people to play, to do their thing before God?

"The belief behind Guardini's assertion is that it is important for us to be natural when we worship, to be most ourselves when we offer our lives to God. And it goes almost without saying that we are most ourselves when we play, when we are caught up both emotionally and physically in what we are engaged at. Even the stuffiest of persons manage to relax somewhat when they are playing, so that their real selves emerge momentarily and have their time in the sun despite the masks of reserve and distance that have been built up through the years."[6]

This self-forgetfulness is only worship's first step, however. We forget ourselves for a while so we can remember Who He is. Our goal is not personal anonymity but the awareness and recognition of His divine presence. In fact, when we know Him as He is and worship Him as we should, we are most fully ourselves. Worship does not make us a nonentity. Never were Adam and Eve more uninhibitedly themselves than when they walked with God in the Garden before the fall. The Scriptures declare, "The man and his wife were both naked, and they felt no shame" (Gen. 2:25). Which is to say that in God's presence, they were fully themselves, totally transparent, and wonderfully alive.

Worship experiences like that are rare indeed. Our conditioning, not to mention our sins and shortcomings, make it difficult for us to come into His presence without shame. Still, from time to time, the reality of Who He is and how He loves us is so totally disarming that we find ourselves naked before Him.

Not long ago I had such an experience, on a Tuesday evening. It was at a special conference where I was scheduled to speak. As I stepped to the pulpit, I was suddenly, overwhelmingly, aware of His presence. Even now, more than six months later, I can hardly speak of it. Like Isaiah in the temple I was "undone" on the inside. Like Moses before the burning bush, I felt as if I were standing on holy ground. Like Elijah on Mount Horeb, I too covered my face.

Wave after wave of His glorious love washed over me and, as it did, I was overcome with weeping. I could not stand. I fell to my knees and pressed my forehead against the floor. His overwhelming holiness was all around me and never have I felt so unclean. Every shortcoming, every failure was shamefully obvious, and yet I did not feel condemned. I felt absolutely unworthy. Yet, as paradoxical as it may sound, I also felt totally accepted.

This went on for more than thirty minutes, though it seemed much shorter than that. During the whole experience, an awesome sense of His presence filled the sanctuary, touching everyone present. The praise singers continued to lead the congregation in worship, and there was an ever-increasing liberty. When I was able to regain my composure, I briefly shared what I could of what I had experienced. Then we began to worship again and never have I experienced anything like it.

As one person, several hundred worshippers praised the Lord. The intensity of our praise was literally overpowering and yet, never has worship been so effortless, so spontaneous. We sang of His holiness and His majesty. We encouraged one another — "Be bold, be strong, for the Lord thy God is with thee." We sang militant songs about spiritual warfare — "I hear the sound of the army of the Lord . . . It's the sound of praise, the sound of war . . . The army of the Lord is marching on."

With each succeeding song, the sense of His presence and power increased. Two or three times we attempted to stop as it was now after 10 P.M. But each time the congregation picked up the song and began to sing again. About 10:30, we were singing "Be Bold" yet again when the trumpet player took off on an inspired solo. He was a recent convert, a former jazz musician, and he just stood there screaming his testimony through that horn. It took very little imagination to see where he had been — years of drug and alcohol abuse had left their scars. He had suffered, there was no doubt about that. But now he was redeemed and his music had a different theme. His joyous celebration held us spellbound at first. Then we were caught up with him in it. We sang and we danced before the Lord with all of our might. It was uninhibited, but it was not disorderly. It was spontaneous, but it was not out of control. It was Spirit-directed. It was worship!

It reminds me of something Walter Wangerin, Jr. wrote in *Ragman and Other Cries of Faith:* ". . . through four states and eight cities we bore the Holy God on our lips, his love in our voices — the Sounds of Grace, gone singing its Thanksgiving.

"Only now, on the afternoon of Thanksgiving Day itself; did all our moods become one mood, and we gazed forward grimly.

Tense, silent, and uncertain. Songs of love had ceased. Falsetto throats had thickened. We were scheduled to sing within the Colorado women's penitentiary.

"Holy, holy, holy. Who suckered us into this?

". . . It wasn't even time, yet, for the concert to begin. No introductions had been made, either by voice or music, and this was not our program. Yet the women were coming, and the practice piece drew a spattering of applause, and Cheryl was lost. By fitful habit she led the choir into another piece for practice, 'Soon and very soon, we are going to meet the king.' Oh, the choir swung hard and speedily against its beat, and Timmy simply hid himself in the solo, and the women laughed at our abandon, and behold: the song itself, it took us over! The nerves left us, and we too began to laugh as we sang, as though there were some huge joke afoot, and we were grateful for the freedom in our throats, and we looked, for the first time, on one another, nodding, slapping another back, singing! And the women took to clapping, some of them dancing with their faces to the floor, their shoulders hunched, and they filled the place with their constant arrival, and some time — no one knew when — the practice turned into an honest concert, but there was no formality to it, because we were free, don't you see, free of the restraints of propriety, free of our fears, free to be truly, truly one with these women, free (Lord, what a discovery!) in prison.

"Song after song, the women stood up and beat their palms together. And they wept, sometimes. Timmy can do that to you. And at one point the entire auditorium, choir and criminals together, joined hands and lifted those hands and rocked and sang, 'Oh, How I Love Jesus.'

"My God, how you do break the bars! How you fling open the doors that imprison and divide us! This is true, for mine eyes have seen it and my heart went out to it: You are so mighty in your mercy."[7]

Sometimes worship like that happens during the message. Remember, the purpose of preaching is not so much to tell you about God as it is to enable you to experience Him for yourself. Sometimes too much information robs an experience of its reality. For instance, there are two ways to see a sunset. First there is the cognitive way. As you watch the sun setting, you compute all the scientific information you can remember — things like how far the earth is from the sun, their relative sizes, how long it takes the earth to revolve around the sun, and, last but not least, the fact that the sun is really not setting at all, the earth is simply rotating on its axis. Now all of that is accurate, even interesting I suppose, but you've just missed the sunset. Most preaching is like that.

In my opinion a better way to view a sunset, or to preach a sermon for that matter, is to focus on the affective dimensions — experience it, touch it, taste it, live it! Not to the exclusion of cognitive considerations, of course, but some things are better caught than taught.

Let me quote G. Robert James who gives us this glimpse of the preaching/worship event.

"All of his (the preacher's) past crystalized into this moment — every experience, every thought, all the love and laughter, all the sorrow and grief, the pain, the loneliness, the hate and woe — and forty-five years of life found its voice and spoke with a haunting, trembling hope.

"His gestures were appropriate, his body language powerfully eloquent, in perfect harmony with the tone of the message. Weariness stooped his shoulders, tension tightened his features, his eyes probed the exposed beams of the sanctuary's ceiling as he described man's search for the invisible God. He spread his arms wide in a gesture of acceptance, extended his hand in invitation, turned just so and every move was reinforced by the tone of his voice, his choice of words and most of all by the touch of God.

"Michael (the preacher) knew, the worshipers realized, they all understood that this was a special time. In the beginning he had struggled, flapping futilely like a bird with a broken wing but now he was soaring like an eagle. At the start the congregation had been lethargic, it was mid-June, the first of the lazy days of summer. But now they were with him, giving as good as they received, limping as he limped, soaring when he soared. This hodgepodge of humanity, all dragging their ratty failures behind them, had somehow become one. One with each other and him, one which was greater than the sum total of all its individual parts.

"They weren't hearing a message, they were living it. He wasn't just preaching, he was the message. The temptation of Adam and Eve was no longer just a bit of biblical symbolism but their own soul's awful moment of truth. They all heard the evil voices, inside of them, outside of them, sometimes whispering, sometimes shouting, 'You shall be gods.' And Adam's guilt and nakedness became theirs for every one of them took the forbidden fruit, played God for a time.

"But Michael did not leave them there, hiding fearful and alone. He led them deeper into the darkness, an eerie noonday darkness, a thick death darkness, an end of the world darkness. And in the darkness they could not see, not even their hands in front of their faces, but they still saw their sins more clearly than ever before. The mad beasts of misspent passions sat upon them, the crippled jackals of moral failure howled hideously and would not be still. When it seemed they could stand no more, when something had to give, they heard a new voice. It was heavy, throbbing, pulsating with pain. And it raised the question none of them dared ask though it screamed ceaselessly inside everyone of them. 'My God, my God, why have you forsaken me?' Nor did Michael leave them in the darkness with the question they dared not ask asked but still unanswered. They followed him into the light where they recognized the nailscarred Christ and his heavy wounded voice. And in the light they saw themselves and one another new. Human still, but new. Wounded and scarred by life, but new. Their weariness was gone but the tired memory lingered giving a poignancy to their appreciation. Guilt and fear, sin and shame all gone, at least for the time being, washed in the brightness of the light. They were speechless, tongue tied, mute and well they might be for what can one say in the midst of a miracle?

"Something had happened they knew that, just what they weren't sure. But they were different, better for the experience, and some of them would never be the same. Not that they would always live on that holy mountain but they would never forget it, always live measuring themselves against its majestic memory."[8]

True worship has the power to do that!

Like the choir and the criminals Wangerin wrote about, like the worshippers James describes, I, too, was changed by my Tuesday night worship experience. I was allowed just a glimpse of His glorious holiness, like Moses on Mount Sinai who was not allowed to see God's face ". . . for there shall no man see me, and live" (Ex. 33:20 KJV), but he was allowed, in the language of the King James text, ". . . (to) see my (God's) back parts" (Ex. 33:23). It was enough to undo me. In the light of His presence, all my righteousness was obviously nothing more than filthy rags. Yet for all of that, I did not feel humiliated or put in my place. In fact, I have never felt so privileged, howbeit, I was left strangely humbled and determined to live the rest of my life in such a way so as not to disgrace that holy moment. That, I believe, is the ultimate consequence of true worship — a changed life and a renewed commitment.

Footnotes

1. Charles Hembree, *Pocket of Pebbles* (Grand Rapids: Baker Book House, 1969), p. 33.

2. Walt Whitman, quoted in *Strength From Shadows*, by R. Earl Allen (Nashville: Broadman Press, 1967), p. 27.

3. John Killinger, *For God's Sake, Be Human* (Waco: Word Books, 1970), p. 18.

4. Kushner, p. 78.

5. Killinger, p. 122.

6. Ibid., p. 122.

7. Walter Wangerin, Jr., quoted in *Disciplines For The Inner Life* by Bob Benson and Michael W. Benson, p. 330.

8. G. Robert James, *Michael* (an unpublished work), pp. 179-182.

Chapter 8

CELEBRATING LIFE

In the last chapter we got a glimpse of what corporate worship can be. Unfortunately, the truth of the matter is that for the most part, worship is not like that. Usually, it is meaningful but definitely not awesome, and sometimes it is downright pedestrian. There are things that we can do to enhance the reality of worship, to be sure. Still, by and large, it is a mystery. The wind of God's Spirit ". . . blows wherever it pleases. You hear its sound, but you cannot tell where it comes from or where it is going . . ." (John 3:8).

Which is not to say that we are absolved from all responsibility, for we are not. Worship cannot be forced, but it can and must be encouraged. While His presence cannot be manufactured, we must learn to recognize His nearness and to accommodate His manifestations. It is up to us to prepare our hearts and minds for His coming. This is the true purpose of the liturgy. Initially, it is not worship, but a discipline which prepares us to worship. It is, according to the prophet, ". . . a sacrifice of praise . . ." (Jer. 33:11 KJV), an act of our will which sensitizes us to His nearness. True worship only happens when we "see" God.

Let me illustrate. Several years ago, a friend of mine boarded a small airliner in a rural airport in southeastern Colorado. Sitting directly in front of him was a young mother and her small son. The child was probably two or three years old. He was properly fascinated by his new surroundings. The seat belts were mechanical marvels to be figured out. Briefcases and other small pieces of luggage were treasures he determinedly tried to reach. All in all, the young mother quite obviously had her hands full. To complicate the situation, she was trying to persuade him to wave good-bye to his daddy.

First she asked, then she tried coaxing, and finally she ordered him. All to no avail. The boy's attention could not be diverted from his new and exciting world of gadgets and strangers.

Having exhausted all civilized means of persuasion, the young mother resorted to force. Wrapping one arm around his middle, she firmly grasped his arm, midway between his elbow and his hand. Turning him toward the window, she began clumsily waving "bye" with his stiff arm.

The boy was a fighter, I'll give him that. Although she outweighed him by almost a hundred pounds, he squirmed and twisted until he managed to jerk his arm free. The victory was a small one and short-lived. The end was inevitable. With renewed determination, his mother took hold of him, pressed his face close to the plane's small window and forced his reluctant arm to wave a mechanical good-bye.

Suddenly, everything changed! Pressing his face against the small window, he cried excitedly, "Daddy! I see Daddy!" He was waving both chubby arms eagerly, almost frantically.

Now let's apply that principle to worship. The worship leader, like the boy's mother, directs us in "acts" of worship. They are designed to wrestle our attention away from the distractions of the world. It's almost as if he were pressing our faces against the window of eternity. At first we don't "see" anything, but because of his enthusiasm we continue to pray and sing, we continue to go through the motions of worship. Suddenly, in the midst of the ritual, we catch sight of God, and our mechanical motions are transformed into reality, into true worship. Now His presence is undeniable, and our hearts, without further prompting, respond of their own accord.

As magnificent as such moments are, that is not all there is to it. <u>Worship doesn't cease when we leave the sanctuary, at least it shouldn't.</u> What happens at church is designed to sensitize us to His presence in our everyday world. It tunes us to the Eternal. We see the world through new eyes. We listen to life with new ears, and, to our amazement, we discover that God is everywhere present. Or as Fredrick Buechner says in "Wishful Thinking," ". . . church isn't the only place where the holy happens. Sacramental moments can occur at any moment, any place, and to anybody. Watching something get born. Making love. A high-school graduation. Somebody coming to see you when you're sick. A meal with people you love. Looking into a stranger's eyes and finding out he's not a stranger. If we weren't blind as bats, we might see that life itself is sacramental."[1]

Several years ago, Brenda and I had just such a sacramental moment. We were eating fried chicken from a fast-food place, while sitting cross-legged in the living room with our backs against a roll of carpet. Even now, as I write about it, something of the feeling comes back. It was a mixture of physical exhaustion and a sense of accomplishment. Night and day, for the better part of three weeks, we had poured ourselves into that run-down rented house, and finally it was starting to feel like home. Swallowing one last bite of chicken, I leaned back against the roll of carpet and wiped my hands on my soiled jeans. It was one of those rare moments — a true serendipity, and I felt fulfilled in a deeply satisfying way.

I looked at Brenda and realized again how blessed I was. She had committed her life to me, holding nothing back. Without a complaint, she had followed me from one struggling church to another. She was my closest friend and lover, the mother of my daughter. That afternoon, she was wearing jeans and a T-shirt.

Her hair was a mess and there was a smudge of paint on her cheek. Still, she had never looked better, and I loved her more than I can say.

The sound of children's laughter drifted in from somewhere down the street. In the distance a dog barked, and I belatedly realized that God was with us. I'm not sure where that thought came from, but suddenly it was there, full-blown and as clear as any thought I've ever had. In a strange sort of way, that unfinished living room became a sanctuary, chicken and corn-on-the-cob, a holy meal, and our conversation a kind of prayer. I know I'm not saying it very well, but for the life of me, I can't get it into words. Still, if you've ever had a moment like that, I don't need to. You already know what I'm talking about. And if you don't, words won't help anyway.

Where is God in all of this? Why, just where He's supposed to be — in the thick of it! For, at the heart of it is God manifesting Himself in life's ordinariness. A child, born in a dung-infested sheep shed to peasant parents. Shepherds stumbling all over themselves in their excitement to answer the angelic summons. An old man — a priest — seeing his dreams, and the dreams of all the ages fulfilled in a baby that for all the world looks just like any other baby. It's God doing what He's always done, doing what He does best — coming to us in the birth of a child, the joy of common men, or even the toothless musings of an old priest.

Now before you decide I've lost my mind or committed a sacrilege, take a minute and remember how often God revealed Himself to ordinary people in the most ordinary appearing ways. The best known, of course, is the Incarnation — "The Word became flesh and lived . . . among us" (John 1:14). God incognito!

To the busy innkeeper, Jesus was just another baby. I'm not sure if that poor man ever realized any different. To the two despairing disciples on the road to Emmaus, He was just a stranger, and an unusually uninformed one at that. He spent an entire day in their company before they realized who He was. To Peter and his fishing buddies, He was just a beachcomber squatting beside a breakfast fire in the early morning mist. Only later, after He called to them, did they recognize Him as the Lord.

What am I trying to say? Just this: "Listen to your life. See it for the fathomless mystery it is. In the boredom and pain of it no less than in the excitement and gladness: touch, taste, smell your way to the holy and hidden heart of it because in the last analysis all moments are key moments, and life itself is grace."[2] Do that, and you will find Him even when you are sure He is nowhere to be found. Miss those "little" moments, and you will be the poorer for it no matter how faithful you are to the house of the Lord.

In his little book, *Now And Then,* Buechner explains it like this: "By examining as closely and candidly as I could the life that had come to seem to me in many ways a kind of trap or dead-end street, I discovered that it really wasn't that at all. I discovered that if you really keep your eye peeled to it and your ears open, if you really pay attention to it, even such a limited and limiting life . . . opens up onto extraordinary vistas. Taking your children to school and kissing your wife good-bye, eating lunch with a friend, trying to do a decent day's work, hearing the rain patter against the window. There is not an event so commonplace but that God is present within it, always hidden, always leaving you room to recognize him, but all the more fascinatingly because of that, all the more compellingly and hauntingly."[3]

I had one of those "hauntingly" special moments when I dedicated Steve and Gwen's baby. Let me hasten to say that every baby dedication is special, but this one more so than most. There were several reasons for that, I suppose. Steve and I are close friends and have been for several years. Therefore, anything which touches him in a special way also touches me. Gwen, too, is a dear friend, and she was so obviously moved by the whole experience that it couldn't help but move me. But I'm getting ahead of myself, so let me go back and start at the beginning.

Steve and Gwen are among the 3.5 million American couples who suffer from infertility. Like most infertile couples, they struggled with feelings of frustration and inadequacy. It was difficult for them to avoid the conclusion that there was something seriously wrong with them, that they were somehow flawed. As time passed and medical science proved increasingly ineffective, they felt more and more helpless. Still they persisted, determined not to leave any stone unturned. If there was a chance that medical science could help them have a baby of their own, they were determined to find it.

It has been observed that no one other than a cancer patient so willingly subjects themselves to so many and so radical a series of medical treatments. Perhaps this, more than any other one thing, reveals how deeply the childless suffer, and how desperately they desire to give birth.

In March, 1986, Steve and I flew to Alaska for a series of meetings. Our first stop was Fairbanks. We arrived, after flying for more than fourteen hours, just in time for our first service. It lasted until almost midnight and when we finally made it back to our room, we were totally exhausted. Early the next morning, the telephone awakened us. It was Gwen, and did she have some news! A friend of theirs, a doctor, was delivering an illegitimate child. The teenage mother wanted to give it up for adoption. The baby was theirs if they wanted it.

They had discussed the possibility of adopting, but only briefly. Now they had to make a decision in a matter of hours, and they were separated by more than five thousand miles. After several hours of prayer, discussion and no little agony, they decided to proceed with the adoption. Steve caught a flight home, and two days later they were the proud parents of a beautiful baby daughter.

If that wasn't a miracle, it was the next best thing. For sure it was an answer to our prayers. When I faced Steve and Gwen and asked them, as the first step in the fulfillment of their charge, to repeat after me the dedicatory prayer from First Samuel 1:27

and 28 (KJV), it was a poignant moment, heavy with long-repressed emotions. "For this child I prayed . . . ." They could hardly get the words out, the joy of their overflowing hearts choked them. I paused to allow them to regain their composure. We started again, ". . . and the Lord hath given me my petition . . ." By now Gwen was weeping unashamedly and, maybe for the first time, I realized, I mean really realized, how she had suffered. This moment belonged to her and God. It was the culmination of her hopes and dreams, an answer to her desperate prayers.

Steve was moved, too, we all were, for all of us, each in our own way, had shared both her anguish and her joy. We, too, knew about weeping in the night, lonely desperation, and the silence of God. Her baby became our answer, as well, and for the length of that dedication all was right with the world. Later, our fears would come back, but not with the same debilitating power. Now we had the wonder of that experience to use against them, the evidence of God's faithfulness. He would see our tears, He would be touched with our bitter cries, He would give us the desperate desires of our hearts too!

When I took the baby in my arms to pray the dedicatory prayer, I felt a new rush of emotion. Like a vision, I saw all the various facets of parenting. I saw the pain and frustration as well as the joy — nothing is more devastating to a young mother than seeing her baby suffer, especially when the baby is too small to tell you where it hurts. Even when healthy, a baby's needs are insatiable. The most committed mother can feel overwhelmed at times, even resentful. Marriage experts call the birth of the first child a predictable crisis. I found myself praying that all the changes, coming at once and so unexpectedly, would not rob Steve and Gwen of the wonder of parenting.

I prayed that they might be sensitive enough to enjoy each moment to the fullest. So many of us are so intent upon preparing for the future that we frequently miss the joy of the present. It's not hard to do. Aletha Jane Lindstrom says, "One spring morning, I paused beside a park fountain to watch the spray diffuse sunlight into shimmering rainbows. A young mother, followed by a tiny blond girl, came hurrying along the path. When the child saw the fountain, she threw her arms wide. 'Mommy, wait!' she cried. 'See all the pretty colors!'

"The mother reached for her daughter's hand. 'Come on,' she urged. 'We'll miss our bus!' Then, seeing the joy on the small face, she relented. 'All right,' she said. 'There'll be another bus soon.'

"As she knelt with her arms around the child, joy filled the mother's face too — that rare and special joy of sharing something lovely with someone we love."[4]

Dedicating Steve and Gwen's baby was, for me, an experience not unlike that moment shared by the young mother and her blond daughter. I knew the joy of sharing something lovely with someone I loved, and I had the added joy of knowing that God shared it as well. This, too, is worship — enjoying the wonder of life with each other and with God!

Sometimes God comes in tragedies as well. When He does, even that tragedy becomes redemptive, it gives life a special poignancy. One woman put it this way: "A diagnosis of cancer . . . is a powerful stimulus against procrastinating on warm and kindly or beautiful things . . . a reminder that many of the material things aren't all that urgent after all . . . Take time to watch the sunset with someone you love; there may not be another as lovely for the two of you."[5]

This, I think, is what John Killinger had in mind when he wrote: "I am reminded of a man who died in my parish once, just a few days before the holidays. He had been ill for many years and was in and out of the hospital frequently. The first words his wife said when I arrived at the house were, 'I am so happy. He won't suffer any more.' Her eyes and cheeks were glossed by tears, but, even in her sorrow, she was glad."[6]

He goes on to say, "And I recall the visage of a man in the hospital who had just been told that his wife had died. 'This too is life,' he said. I have thought of those words many times. Somehow, joy arises from loss and suffering and toil as much as it does from pleasure and ease. It is much deeper than the surface of existence; it has to do with the whole structure of life. It is the perfume of the rose that is crushed, the flash of color in the bird that is hit, the lump in the throat of the man who sees and knows, instinctively, that life is a many splendored thing."[7]

Don't misunderstand me. I am not suggesting that God sends adversity to enhance our appreciation of life or to make us more aware of His nearness. Nor am I implying that the fullness of life comes only to those who have passed through deep waters. Rather, I am saying that God is present in all of life, including its tragedies. His presence transforms even these agonizing experiences into opportunities for worship.

In one day, Job lost everything — his servants, his livestock, his wealth and his children. "At this, Job got up and tore his robe and shaved his head. Then he fell to the ground in worship and said: 'Naked I came from my mother's womb, and naked I will depart. The Lord gave and the Lord has taken away; may the name of the Lord be praised.' In all this, Job did not sin by charging God with wrongdoing" (Job 1:20-22).

We don't worship God because of our losses, but in spite of them. We don't praise Him for the tragedies, but in them. Like Job, we hear God speak to us out of the storm. (Job 38:1.) Like the disciples at sea in a small boat, caught in a severe storm, we too see Jesus coming to us in the fourth watch of the night. We hear Him say, "Take courage! It is I. Don't be afraid" (Matt. 14:27).

Robert Louis Stevenson, in one of his beautiful stories, relates how a ship was being buffeted by a terrible storm. One sailor disobeyed the captain's order and made his way across the deck to the foredeck, and up to the pilot's wheel. There the pilot had been tied to the mast in order that the fury of the wind could not dislodge him. Strapped to the pole behind him, and with a confident grasp on the wheel in front of him, the pilot turned for a moment and smiled at the frightened sailor. The sailor returned to the fearful crew and assured them that everything was all right. "I have seen the pilot's face, and he was smiling."[8]

This past week, I ministered to a young man whose mother just had a radical mastectomy. The prognosis was not very encouraging, and for the first time in his life he came face to face with the reality that one day his parents would die. As I listened to him work through this anxiety, I couldn't help reliving a very similar experience. I remember thinking, it's sobering when you realize for the first time that your parents aren't going to live forever. Theoretically, I've known that for years, but it really sank home two years ago when my seemingly indestructible father was stricken with heart disease.

Dad underwent two major surgeries in the space of three weeks. The first was double by-pass, open-heart surgery. Then, three weeks, later, he had his gall bladder removed. I wasn't able to get a flight until late evening, and it was well past ten o'clock when I finally made it to the hospital. Dad acknowledged my presence, but that was about all he could manage before succumbing to the pain medication. About midnight, I left Mother to her bedside vigil and drove "home" to the house where I grew up.

Opening the trunk to get my bag, I saw Dad's toolbox and coveralls — symbols of his strength and resourcefulness. There wasn't anything he couldn't fix. In the living room I encountered his favorite chair, a lazy-boy recliner covered in a wool plaid. Now, it became a haunting symbol of his sickness. How many nights had he spent here, unable to sleep, alone with the darkness and his pain?

A deep sadness settled over me. I tried to reason it away. I was tired and lonely, the house was empty. My sadness wasn't fooled. I was face to face with my own mortality and Dad's.

I was tired but couldn't sleep, so I wandered through the empty house listening to the stillness. How different from my childhood when four kids created a constant commotion. How different from other trips home, holidays and vacations when the house rang with laughter, love, and grandchildren were everywhere underfoot. I sat in Dad's favorite chair and cried. I couldn't help it.

Yet even in my sadness, there was much to be thankful for. Dad and I had shared on a deeper level than we had known before. We didn't want a single affirming word unshared, any feeling of love unexpressed. I remembered holding his hand the day before his open-heart surgery and the closeness we felt. The way he blinked to hold back his tears when he told me all the things he had wanted to do for Mother and hadn't got to, at least not yet. Some improvements on the house and a trip to Hawaii. After a while, he had fallen asleep, and I was left with my thoughts and the realization of how much I loved that special man I call Dad. Yet, even in my sorrow, I realized anew that life's tribulations too can be a source of spiritual richness if a person has a lifetime of shared experiences to draw upon.

Alone in the house that night, I had a choice. I could either entertain my fears or my memories. I chose the latter. The first thing that came to mind was something I had been told rather than anything of which I had a conscious memory. My dad has always been an avid reader. When I was just a baby, I would sit in his lap, perfectly still, for hours while he read. Now, sitting in his favorite chair with a stack of books at my elbow, I thought of that and realized that my own love for books might very well have been born right there in his arms. Even today I think of a good book as a trusted friend, and I associate them with happiness and love. Is it not possible that those warm feelings are a carry-over of the love and security I found in his arms?

Then my mind leaped ahead twenty years. Brenda and I were pastoring a small church in Florence, Colorado. It was nearly 1,100 miles from Houston, yet, without fail, Dad and Mom made a flying trip to see us every major holiday. Usually, they had to drive all night, both coming and returning home. They came for Leah's first Christmas. She was only seven months old, and Brenda dressed her in striped pajamas and a tiny Santa's cap. My family arrived about 2:00 A.M. on Christmas morning. Immediately, we exchanged gifts, after lots of kisses and hugs, that is. Later that day, we went ice skating on a pond swept clean of snow by bitterly cold winds, high in the Rockies. Then we took turns riding a toboggan down the mountainside at speeds no one in their right mind would ever attempt. Miraculously, no one was hurt, and we returned to the house for Christmas leftovers and childhood memories, relived with a relish known only to happy families.

Back again my mind went to my childhood. This time to the night I was called to preach. I was barely thirteen and when I told Dad what had happened, he gave me just enough affirmation to let me know how proud he was, but not nearly enough to make me think more highly of myself than I should have. Then he gave me some of the wisest counsel I've ever received. He told me to keep that call a secret between the two of us. When I started preaching or began preparation for the ministry, that would be time enough to make it public. I accepted his counsel that night without question, because I trusted him. Now I see the wisdom in what he said. If my call had turned out to be nothing but an emotional experience and I had already announced it, I might have felt obligated to continue, just to save face.

Through junior high I always played sports — football and basketball, especially. I wasn't really much of an athlete. Second string was the best I could manage. Still, Dad stopped at practice every night on his way home from work. We played our games on Saturday mornings. He saw to it that the whole family was in attendance even though the chances were pretty good I wouldn't get to play. Never once did he make me feel like I wasn't living up to his expectations. With him, I was always an All-Stater!

This reliving of the past went on all night long as I tossed fitfully, unable to sleep, with only God and my memories to keep me company. Along about dawn, I realized that even if Dad died, I couldn't be angry, not really. The thirty-eight years we had shared had enough love and laughter for two or three lifetimes. No one could ever take Dad's place. I understood that better than ever now, but I would always have the memories and the God he made more real to me than life.

That morning I decided to celebrate life rather than grieve, and when I did I realized that the Lord of life was present and celebrating with me! Dad recovered from his surgeries and is still alive today, two years later. But I know now how to prepare for that inevitable moment we must all face. When Dad finally goes the way of all flesh, I am not going to grieve over what might have been, rather I am going to thank God for what we had. I'm going to celebrate life! Dad would want it that way. That doesn't mean I won't grieve, or that I won't miss him. It just means he can't ever be totally gone as long as I have the memories of the life he so freely shared with me and all of his family.

Footnotes

1. Frederick Buechner, "Wishful Thinking," *Disciplines For The Inner Life* by Bob Benson and Michael W. Benson p. 201.

2. Ibid., p. 120.

3. Frederick Buechner, *Now and Then, Disciplines For The Inner Life* by Bob Benson and Michael W. Benson, p. 120.

4. Aletha Jane Lindstrom, "A Legacy of Rainbows," *Reader's Digest*, Dec. 1984, p. 122.

5. "Taking Time" (U.S. Department of Health and Human Services, NIH Publication No. 82-2059, Reprinted Sept. 1982), p. VII.

6. Killinger, p. 147.

7. Ibid., p. 147.

8. R. Earl Allen, *Trials, Tragedies, and Triumphs* (Westwood: Fleming H. Revell, 1965), p. 96.

Chapter 9

THE SINGERS OF LIFE

When we met, I was just a young preacher, not yet dry behind the ears as they say, and pastoring my first church. My friend was in his mid-thirties, divorced and starting over. Finally I managed to work up my courage, and I asked him to tell me about it. For what seemed like an awfully long time, he didn't say anything. Distinctly, I remember the wheezing of the old floor furnace as it fought to hold its own against the December night. Outside, the wind moaned through the leafless trees, causing them to crack and pop in the cold.

At last he spoke, in a voice I had to strain to hear.

"It was the worst day of my life and when the judge said, 'Divorce granted.' I wanted to die. It wasn't a shock. Not like two years earlier when I discovered she was involved with a member of my congregation. That was a shock — like hearing the doctor tell you that you have cancer. This was more final — like a death. Up until then I had managed to hang onto a desperate hope. Not that she had ever given me any reason to believe she would change her mind, for she hadn't. Still I couldn't bring myself to accept the fact that our marriage was over. I kept expecting an eleventh-hour reprieve. With the judge's words, my last hope died.

"I can remember standing on the courthouse steps as she drove off with our four kids. They cried and waved, but she never even looked back. Walking toward my four-year-old sedan, I remember thinking that everything in the world that I loved was gone. Not just my family, but my church as well. The District Superintendent thought it would be better for everyone concerned if we would make a clean break and not leave any unpleasant reminders. Without a second thought, he removed me from the church I had planted six years earlier and reassigned me to this three point charge (a rural pastorate consisting of three churches). It was like adding insult to injury.

"Somehow I found my car and started driving. I ended up in the Garden of the Gods National Park. Since the tourist season hadn't really started, I had it mostly to myself. I found a remote spot and parked. At last the tears came. Silently at first, then great gasping sobs that shook my whole body. Wave after wave of grief swept over me, and I was powerless to stop it. After a while, I found myself walking — aimlessly among the towering boulders. Thoughts of suicide flirted on the edges of my mind, wooed me, tempted me with promises of a painless oblivion.

"In desperation I began to sing. At first it was hardly more than a strangled whisper.

" 'Rock of ages, cleft for me.
Let me hide myself in thee.'[1]

"Then with more faith:

" 'What a friend we have in Jesus,
all our sins and griefs to bear . . .
In his arms he'll take and shield thee,
Thou wilt find a solace there.'[2]

"I climbed to the top of a huge rock and sang at the top of my lungs, almost in defiance of my pain and despair. Hymn after hymn came to me, and I sang until my throat was raw.

" 'There's not a friend like the lowly Jesus,
No not one. No not one.'[3]

"And:

" 'I come to the garden alone
while the dew is still on the roses;
And the voice I hear, falling on my ear, The Son of
God discloses.

" 'And He walks with me, and He talks with me,
And He tells me I am His own,
And the joy we share as we tarry there,
None other has ever known.'[4]

"Nothing had really changed yet everything was different. The afternoon was gone. The first stars were materializing against the darkening sky as I carefully climbed down and made my way to the car. I learned something that day, something about worship. It has an amazing power to renew the soul. Without it, I don't know if I would have made it."

His voice trailed off and we sat for a long time, each of us immersed in our own thoughts. That night and his story have come back to me many times during the past twenty years, especially in times of tragedy. Like him, I, too, have come to realize that worship is an act of faith, not infrequently in the face of overwhelming odds. An act which renews the worshipper and often enables him to overcome the most impossible circumstances.

His experience does, however, raise at least a couple of questions. First, how does a person worship when all hope is gone, when life is totally undone? And secondly, how does worship work? I mean how did singing a few hymns restore his sense of purpose, his life's direction?

Jesus told a parable which may shed some light on the first question. " '. . . Suppose one of you has a friend, and he goes to him at midnight and says, "Friend, lend me three loaves of bread, because a friend of mine on a journey has come to me, and I have nothing to set before him." Then the one inside answers, "Don't bother me. The door is already locked, and my children are with me in bed. I can't get up and give you anything." I tell you, though he will not get up and give him the bread because he is his friend, yet because of the man's persistence he will get up and give him as much as he needs' " (Luke 11:5-8).

"Don't be fooled, this is more than just a story. It is life laid bare by the one who understands it best. He's warning us, telling us, that sooner or later life is going to surprise us with some unexpected demands. He does not hint as to what form they will take but experience suggests a number of possibilities: delinquency, divorce, a business failure, a crippling accident, a terminal illness, death? Not necessarily to us, but in ways that affect us.

"This host provided because he was resourceful. He did not sit down and wring his hands in despair, he took action. Through the dark streets, through the narrow, unmarked alleys he journeys until he reaches, at last, a house familiar, even in the dark. He pounds on the door, he makes his situation known, he begs bread.

"How did he know where to go? Why was he so sure this friend had bread? We can assume that he has been here before, that this is a familiar friend, one whose hospitality he has enjoyed on frequent occasions. Does he not remember his friend's table groaning beneath its burden of bread, his friend's cupboard about to burst with its abundance? This is no shot in the dark. It's a plea based on experience.

"What will we do in the midnight of our need, when the light of life is gone, when our personal cupboards are despairingly bare?

"Any conclusion here is speculation, to be sure, but let me suggest that a familiarity with prayer's pathway to God will increase one's ability to find Him in the darkness. If we have come often to God in the sunshine of our lives, our anxious feet will find the familiar pathway, even in the darkest night. Though blinded by disaster, though hounded and hindered by doubt, though confused by life which seems out of hand, we can find our way to God intuitively because going to Him has become second nature, a way of life."[5]

Like the empty-handed host in Jesus' parable, my friend also knew where to find God. Although blinded by despair, the disciplines of a lifetime enabled him to worship. Out of some half-forgotten place in his childhood came a hymn. Songs that seemed so sentimental to a rambunctious teenager now returned with power and clarity. Worship, which in the sanctuary had seemed like so much ritual, now rose from his innermost being and affirmed the greatness of God. And with that act, he began the long journey back.

If you've lived for any length of time, you've probably had opportunity to see the different ways people respond to adversity. The same tragedy can make one person better and another person bitter. What makes the difference? Resources. Inner resources developed across a lifetime through spiritual disciplines. If you haven't worshipped regularly in the sunshine of your life, you probably won't be able to worship in the darkness. If you haven't been intimate with God in life's ordinariness, it's not likely that you will know how or where to find Him should life hand you some real hardships. But by the same token, if you have worshipped often and regularly, then you will undoubtedly worship well in the hour of your greatest need.

Frederick Buechner gives us a glimpse of such worship in "A Room Called Remember." He writes, "When the worst finally happens, or almost happens, a kind of peace comes. I had passed beyond grief, beyond terror, all but beyond hope, and it was there, in that wilderness, that for the first time in my life I caught sight of something of what it must be like to love God truly. It was only a glimpse, but it was like stumbling on fresh water in the desert, like remembering something so huge and extraordinary that my memory had been unable to contain it. Though God was nowhere to be clearly seen, nowhere to be clearly heard, I had to be near him — even in the elevator riding up to her floor, even walking down the corridor to the one door among all those doors that had her name taped on it. I loved him because there was nothing else left. I loved him because he seemed to have made himself as helpless in his might as I was in my helplessness. I loved him not so much in spite of there being nothing in it for me but almost because there was nothing in it for me. For the first time in my life, there in that wilderness, I caught what it must be like to love God truly, for his own sake, to love him no matter what. If I loved him with less than all my heart, soul, might, I loved him with at least as much of them as I had left for loving anything."[6]

Maybe what I'm trying to say is that now is the time to worship, this day and every day. It's not an activity reserved for Sundays at 11 A.M.; not something requiring sermon and song, not even stained glass. It's not discipline as much as it is aptitude. You can't force a person to admire beauty. It just happens. So it is with worship — let him who has eyes to see, see.

For the seeing person all of life is a sanctuary resplendent with the presence of God. A rain-wet flower backlighted by the setting sun is as inspiring as any religious symbol, perhaps more so. A meadowlark's clear song, be it early morning or late evening, is as fine a call to prayer as any man could ever hope to hear. For the apartment dweller, locked behind his glass and concrete walls, it may be something as common as raindrops on a window pane or the smell of supper cooking on the stove. Let him who has eyes to see, see!

There is a story of a peasant shepherd who was grazing his sheep when he noticed a wildflower of unusual beauty. Turning aside to study it in more detail, he decided to pick it. It was different from anything he had ever seen, and he was sure the other shepherds would want to see it.

As soon as he picked it, the whole hillside opened up revealing a cave filled with chests of precious stones, silver and gold. For a moment he stood transfixed, then he rushed into the cave and began to fill his pockets. As he turned to go, heavy-laden with his new-found wealth, he heard a voice. It said simply, "Don't forget the best."

Quickly he emptied his pockets and rummaged through the chests of precious stones, searching for the "best" gem. To his untrained eye, they all appeared about the same so once more he filled his pockets and turned to go. The voice, again, "Don't forget the best."

Once more he made a thorough search. Somewhere there must be a prize gem or a special piece of jewelry. No luck. They all looked the same to him. As he headed for the cave's entrance, weighted down with his new-found wealth, the voice stopped him in his tracks a third time. "Don't forget the best." He had a troubling sense that he was somehow making a terrible mistake, but for the life of him, he couldn't imagine what it might be.

Ignoring the voice, he walked into the sunlight. As he did, the earth trembled, and he turned just in time to see the hillside closing. The last thing he saw was the beautiful wildflower, discarded in his mad scramble to fill his pockets. Then he understood. The flower was the best. To his consternation, he found all his gems had turned to dust. Without the "best" they too were worthless!

Now, I'm sure you realize that that is not a true story in the sense that it really happened. Yet we all know that some things are true even if they didn't happen, and this is one of them. For it is true — the best things in life are free. Unfortunately, the world system seduces us. Soon we have forgotten the things that made us happy, the things that made life meaningful. We discard them, without a backward glance, like the shepherd casting aside the wildflower. And like him, we often realize it only after it's too late.

Take a moment now and remember the flowers in your life, those special little things that give life its meaning, those moments that call you to worship. Early morning prayer in a dim sanctuary is such a time for me, as is a good book or a few minutes alone at the end of a busy day. Sometimes at night, when I lie in bed beside Brenda, I am simply overcome with thankfulness, and I praise God for the gift of marriage and family.

The sound of Leah's laughter, half a house away, can take me back to the less hectic days when she was just a toddler. I see

Having the Holy Ghost

her again in a blue flannel pajama top and wool knee socks, nothing else. I'm transfixed for a moment, and I worship again thanking God for the miracle of birth. Looking back, I'm so grateful for the fourteen years of ministry in rural areas. The pace was less hectic, the demands of ministry minimal. During Leah's formative years, I got to spend lots of time with her. Occasionally, I chafed at the bit, but now I'm grateful for the family times it afforded. I wouldn't trade all the success in the world for the memories we made and the relationships we built. Let him who has eyes to see, see!

Harold Kushner writes: "In a world where not everyone will do great deeds or achieve great success, God has given us the capacity to find greatness in the everyday. Lunch can be a hurried refueling, the equivalent of an auto racer's pit stop, or it can be an opportunity to savor the miracle that dirt, rain, seeds, and human imagination can work on our taste buds. We just have to be wise enough to know how to recognize the miracle, and not rush headlong past it in our search for 'something important.' We can smile at the adolescent girl mooning over her new boyfriend. She may think that the most wonderful thing in human history has just happened to her, while we know it is just another set of glands ripening on schedule and in six months she will wonder what she ever saw in him. Yet there is something touching about being able to be made so happy by a letter, a phone call, or a smile. There is a capacity for finding joy in the ordinary which we might well envy. The good life, the truly human life is based not on a few great moments but on many, many little ones. It asks of us that we relax in our quest long enough to let those moments accumulate and add up to something."[7]

Can we return to my friend for a moment? He survived his divorce, and today he is an effective pastor of a significant congregation. I would hate to think what might have happened if worship had not been a way of life for him. What would have sustained him? How would he have made it? He was able to worship in the dark night of his soul because he was a practiced worshipper. For him, all of life was a sanctuary and each experience an invitation to celebrate his faith.

Another question his experience raises is, "How does worship work?" That is, how does it renew our spirits and restore our faith? The answer, I believe, lies in the power of presence and perspective. Let me share a story which I think will illustrate my point.

Late one Sunday night, I received a phone call informing me that Chuck had died suddenly of a heart attack, leaving a wife and two teenaged children. I was only twenty-three at the time, and this was really my first encounter with sudden death. Somehow I managed to say the right things, and before I knew it, I was dressed and out the door.

Driving through the night toward their home, I was frightened. A choir of depressing voices sang a dreadful doubt-filled harmony, and I was plagued with an overwhelming feeling of incompetency. I was the pastor. I was supposed to have the answers, or so I thought. Somehow I was expected to enter their shattered world and dismiss the darkness of death.

Everything I thought of sounded trite, memorized, terribly insufficient. I prayed desperately, but still I had no idea what I was going to do. I parked the car and approached the house with real apprehension.

The doorbell was answered almost before I got my finger off the button. A neighbor directed me to the dining room where the family was seated around an oval-shaped table. With absolutely no premeditation, I found myself sitting down and grasping the hands of those on each side of me. Tentatively, I lifted my voice in song. For the first few bars I sang alone, then I was joined by a second voice, and then another and then still another. Finally, all of us were singing through our tears and our pain. First one hymn and then another. And with each succeeding song, we sang with more conviction.

After about thirty minutes, I discovered I was no longer plagued with doubt. I wasn't the only one who felt different, either. The whole family was transformed. Hopelessness gave way to hope, fear yielded to trust, and confusion was replaced by confidence.

The dreaded enemy, death, had been driven out. The Lord of Life was present with peace and comfort.

Don't misunderstand me. I'm not implying that there was no more sorrow, no more pain or loss. Worship did not nullify Chuck's tragic death, but it did put it into perspective. Chuck was not dead, just gone. He was with God and God was with us. We could have focused only on our loss and been devastated. Instead, we chose to take it to the Lord in worship, and we discovered a sufficiency in His grace that was simply unspeakable.

Without God, death is an unequivocal tragedy. Seen in the light of our Lord's resurrection, however, it is reduced to a wound to the living. Painful to be sure, unbearably painful at times, but just a temporary condition. We know that ". . . neither death nor life, neither angels nor demons, neither the present nor the future, nor any powers, neither height nor depth, nor anything else in all creation, will be able to separate us from the love of God that is in Christ Jesus our Lord" (Rom. 8:38,39). And with that hope is the assurance of being reunited with those who have preceded us in death.

Loren Eiseley, anthropologist, shares an experience from the world of nature which illustrates this truth well.

"When I awoke, dimly aware of some commotion and outcry in the clearing, the light was slanting down through the pines in such a way that the glade was lit like some vast cathedral. I could see the dust motes of wood pollen in the long shaft of life, and there on the extended branch sat an enormous raven with a red and squirming nestling in his beak. The sound that awoke me was the outraged cries of the nestling's parents, who flew helplessly in circles about the clearing. The sleek black monster was indifferent to them. He gulped, whetted his beak on the dead branch a moment and sat still. Up to that point the little tragedy had followed the usual pattern. But suddenly, out of all that area of woodland, a soft sound of complaint began to rise. Into the glade fluttered small birds of half a dozen varieties drawn by the anguished outcries of the tiny parents.

"No one dared to attack the raven. But they cried there in some instinctive common misery. The bereaved and the unbereaved. The glade filled with their soft rustling and their cries. They fluttered as though to point their wings at the murderer. There was a dim intangible ethic he had violated, that they knew. He was a bird of death. And he, the murderer, the black bird at the heart of life, sat on there, glistening in the common light, formidable, unmoving, unperturbed, untouchable.

"The sighing died. It was then I saw the judgment. It was the judgment of life against death. I will never see it again so forcefully presented. I will never hear it again in notes so tragically prolonged. For in the midst of protest, they forgot the violence. There, in that clearing, the crystal note of a song sparrow lifted hesitantly in the hush. And finally, after painful fluttering, another took the song, and then another, the song passing from one bird to another, doubtfully at first, as though some evil thing were being slowly forgotten. Till suddenly they took heart and sang from many throats joyously together as birds are known to sing. They sang because life is sweet and sunlight beautiful. They sang under the brooding shadow of the raven. In simple truth they had forgotten the raven, for they were the singers of life, and not of death."[8]

That's how worship works. It recognizes the presence of the Living God in even the most unspeakable tragedies. At first we protest, not against God, though we have been known to blame Him for terrible things (unspeakable things for which He is not responsible), but against the evil thing that has rent our world. Then we grieve, for grief too, is an act of worship, and God grieves with us just as Jesus wept with Mary and Martha when Lazarus died. And finally we sing in praise and adoration for we are children of life and not of death, and our songs are the celebration of life!

Footnotes

1. Augustus M. Toplady and Thomas Hastings, "Rock of Ages," *Hymns of Glorious Praise* (Springfield: Gospel Publishing House, 1969), p. 336.

2. Joseph Scriven and Charles C. Converse, "What a Friend We Have in Jesus," *Hymns of Glorious Praise,* p. 403.

3. Johnson Oatman Jr. and George C. Hugg, "No Not One," *Hymns of Glorious Praise*, p. 481.

4. C. Austin Miles, "In The Garden," *Hymns of Glorious Praise*, p. 304.

5. Richard D. Exley, *The Other God* (Plainfield: Logos International, 1979), pp. 33,34.

6. Frederick Buechner, quoted in *Disciplines For The Inner Life* by Bob Benson and Michael W. Benson, p. 56.

7. Kushner, pp. 109,110.

8. Loren Eiseley, quoted in *Creative Brooding* by Robert Raines (New York: Macmillan, 1966) pp. 36,37.

Part IV

PLAY

Part IV

PLAY

In our work-oriented society, rest and play have gotten a bad name, especially play. That is not to say that we don't play, for we do, but even our play is built around a production mentality. Only certain forms of play are *acceptable*, those that are designed to make us more productive people. And once we buy into that, it's not play anymore but just another kind of work. Play can obviously contribute to our physical and emotional well-being, but that contribution must be a consequence and not a goal. Pure play's only goal is play itself. It is its own reward. If you are ever tempted to doubt that, just spend a hot August afternoon watching the kids in a public swimming pool. That's play at its best.

When I pastored small churches in the Colorado Rockies, play was a regular part of my life. The demands of the ministry were less. The rural lifestyle lent itself to a good balance between work and rest. Unfortunately, after moving to Tulsa, I let play slip until it was no longer a regular part of my life's rhythm. After a time I recognized what was happening and I joined a fitness club, so I would have a place to "play." It was well equipped with racquetball courts, swimming pools, jogging tracks, weight and exercise rooms and tennis courts. At first, things seemed to go pretty well, but bit by bit I fell back into the production mentality.

Soon, I found myself working out instead of playing. In the swimming pool, I pushed myself harder every day. I counted the laps and timed them. It was rigorous, and I was determined to swim longer and faster every week. Then my religious conditioning crept in as well, and I found myself quoting scriptures as I swam, or praying for the pressing needs of the church and those I loved. Now, there's not necessarily anything wrong with that, but it's definitely not play. If you doubt that, just compare my Spartan discipline to the joyous exuberance of the kids in the public pool. Now that's play!

Let me quote from a little book that I found both insightful and extremely helpful. It was written by Tim Hansel and is titled *When I Relax I Feel Guilty.*

"If you will excuse me a moment for not speaking English, I think you will find it helpful to know the background of the word 'leisure.' It comes from the Latin word 'licere,' which means 'to be permitted.' More today than ever, we need to learn how to give ourselves permission to relax, to play, to enjoy life, and to enjoy God for Who He is.

"It's interesting that the Latin word for work was 'negotium,' or 'nonleisure.' Work was thus secondary, defined as it related to leisure. Our society does just the opposite, defining leisure as 'nonwork.' We tend to be almost compulsively utilitarian. Everything must contribute to our work. We play in order to work better or to be more 'useful' to God. In many ways, these are the habits that keep us unhappy. In our myopia of overvalued productivity, we have forgotten how to enjoy things for what they are.

"Leisure is more than just nonwork. It is a point of contact with reality and a catalyst for new experiences, new ideas, new people, and new places. It is the time when the gift of wholeness again becomes a hope and a possibility.

"In order for this to happen, three things must be done. First, we must be convinced of the importance of quality leisure in our lives — not superficial play, but true 'licere' . . . . Second, we must understand how to practice quality leisure. We cannot assume it will just happen. It doesn't. Third, we must then act on what we know to be true. This is both the difficult part and the most exciting. Reading a book on the subject is not enough. We cannot afford to be hearers only. It must be lived."[1]

As we begin this section, let me make two observations. First, I think it is a mistake to define work as *nonleisure*, as the Latin word *negotium* suggests. It is, I think, equally wrong to define leisure as *nonwork*, as our society does. Work and play are both valued elements in the divinely designed rhythm of life. To define them as non-anything is to elevate one above the other, and that is a mistake. In truth, they are equal in value but different in function.

Second, rhythm does not suggest equal amounts but a delicate balance which produces the desired result. We are not contending that our lives should be divided into four equal parts — one for work, rest, worship and play. Rather, we see life as an integrated whole where the divine rhythm of work, rest, worship and play have been personalized to create wholeness. If you are truly sensitive to God and in tune with your own life, then you know better than anyone else how to integrate these elements into your life for maximum benefit. This takes effort, courage, and discipline, and in the case of play, a little craziness. Zorba, in the book *Zorba The Greek*, says, "Boss, you've got everything except one thing — Madness! A man needs a little madness or else he never dares cut the rope to be free."[2]

I couldn't agree more. To play well, to cut the ropes which keep us bound to the rigorous demands of our work-oriented mind-set, we all need a "little madness." In fact, it's our only hope.

Footnotes

1. Tim Hansel, *When I Relax I Feel Guilty* (Elgin: David C. Cook Publishing Co., 1979), pp. 30,31.

2. Nikos Kazantzakis, *Zorba The Greek* (New York: Ballantine Books, 1952), p. 334.

Chapter 10

FREE TO PLAY

When I say "play," what do you think of? What comes to mind?

I see a mental mosaic composed of almost forgotten experiences from my own childhood, plus at least half-a-hundred scenes from across the years. I remember a Christmas morning when I was, maybe, ten. I am lying on my stomach on the bare hardwood floor aiming a cork gun at a row of plastic crows sitting on a fence. But in my mind I'm a grown man with a twelve-gauge and the plastic crows are a covey of quail. This scene fades to be replaced by another. Now I really am a man, and I'm standing in Leah's bedroom door watching her and her friends play Barbies. She's only seven or eight, but when she plays, she can be as old as she wants. On this day she's at least nineteen, beautiful, and in love with Ken. It's just a make-believe world but, for the moment, it is as real as my presence in the doorway, maybe more.

From somewhere, my mind conjures up a rainy afternoon. I see children, boys I think, in yellow slickers and black boots. With deliberate determination they seek out every puddle and stomp through it, splashing water everywhere. They're getting wet, and they will catch it when they get home. But for now, they are lost in a world of mud puddles and laughter.

In the next scene I'm a grown man again, but a boy at heart. I'm wrestling with Jason, my five-year-old nephew. He calls time-out and heads for the kitchen. I hunt a vantage point where I can watch him without being too noticeable. After pulling a chair up to the counter, he amazingly begins to eat leftover spinach from a serving bowl. For a minute I can't believe what I'm seeing; then I remember what I told him at dinner. Taking a big bite of spinach, I had said, "Jason, you will never be able to whip me if you don't eat your spinach." He didn't believe me, but now he does. After several mouthfuls he climbs down, and I slip back into the living room to wait for him. He struts back in, flexing his pipe-stem arms and announces, "Now I'm ready." We wrestle again, and I let him win every match. He goes to bed a confirmed believer in the miraculous power of spinach, and I go to bed a happy man. I've put one over on the kid. Of course, my day will come, but I put that thought out of my mind for the time being. There's more, but I think you get the point.

What did you think of? A friendly tennis match? Water skiing at the lake, a picnic at the park, volleyball in the back yard? If you're the harried mother of three pre-schoolers, you may have thought of toys scattered all over the living room or children fighting. Whatever the case, most of us probably associated play with children, fun, and a freedom from responsibility. You may have even experienced a moment of nostalgic wistfulness when you wished again for the easier, carefree days of childhood. For the times when you played hide and seek in the dark, or had hay fights in the barn or spent lazy summer afternoons lying on your back contemplating nothing more serious than the changing cloud formations passing overhead.

And the chances are pretty good that you felt a little guilty for thinking about it. I mean, what right do we have to entertain ourselves with thoughts of play when the world is filled with so much suffering? To which I would respond that we not only have a right, but a responsibility, not only to think about play but to play. Even Jesus, with His awesome sense of call ("I must work the works of him that sent me . . ." John 9:4 KJV), regularly took time for play. He slipped away to the desert to be alone. He socialized so frequently that the religious leaders accused Him of being a winebibber and a glutton. Why? Because He realized that without the renewal provided by rest and the pleasure derived from play, He would soon become part of the suffering He sought to alleviate. Many a good person, many a compassionate person, has grown cynical simply because they failed to play, they failed to enjoy the life He gives.

Don't misunderstand me. I am not saying that we should play so that we can work more effectively, but that we should play for the sheer pleasure of playing. When God sees us having the time of our lives, it warms His heart. Our pleasure is His pleasure. I think He must feel something like Chuck Swindoll felt the night he wrote:

"Tonight was fun 'n games night around the supper table in our house. It was wild. First of all, one of the kids snickered during the prayer (which isn't that unusual) and that tipped the first domino. Then a humorous incident from school was shared and the event (as well as how it was told) triggered havoc around the table. That was the beginning of twenty to thirty minutes of the loudest, silliest, most enjoyable laughter you can imagine. At one point I watched my oldest literally fall off his chair in hysterics, my youngest doubled over in his chair as his face wound up in his plate with corn chips stuck to his cheeks . . . and my two girls leaning back, lost and preoccupied in the most beautiful and beneficial therapy God ever granted humanity: laughter.

"All is quiet now, a rather unusual phenomenon around here. It's almost midnight and although my bones are weary, I'm filled and thrilled with the most pleasant memories a father can enjoy — a healthy, happy, laughing family. What a treasure! The load that often weighs heavily upon my shoulders about this time each week seems light and insignificant now. Laughter, the needed friend, has paid another dividend."[1]

Is it possible that our laughter can make the load that often weighs heavily upon God's shoulders lighter? As preposterous as it may seem, I believe it can. But that's not the point. We don't need to justify our pleasure or our play. God wills it. He wants us to enjoy ourselves.

You may be remembering a disappointing experience, a time when you really made an effort to play, but there was no pleasure in it. Oh, you laughed when you were supposed to, but it was only a surface laughter. In your heart you kept asking, "Are we having fun yet?" Gritting your teeth, you plunged ahead. You were going to have fun if it killed you, and it almost did.

Perhaps you were trying too hard. Fun can't be forced. Maybe you were operating on someone else's agenda, trying to make their play work for you. That's no good either. One man's play is another man's work. Let me give you some hints for getting started.

First, you must be totally convinced that play is an important priority, deserving the same time and attention that you devote to work, rest and worship. Nothing kills fun faster than a guilty conscience. If all you can think about is the work you should be doing, then you will be hard-pressed to play well. To really play, you have to throw yourself into it, give it all you've got.

Don't misunderstand me. I'm not advocating a pleasure-seeking, hedonistic lifestyle. Rather, I'm trying to give wholesome play its proper place. The wise man wrote, "There is a time for everything, and a season for every activity under heaven: . . . a time to weep and a time to laugh, a time to mourn and a time to dance . . . I know that there is nothing better for men than to be happy and do good while they live. That every man may eat and drink, and find satisfaction . . . this is the gift of God" (Eccl. 3:1,4,12,13).

After you have settled the issue intellectually, even after you are convinced that the Scriptures teach that play is a gift from God, to be received with thanksgiving and enjoyed, you will still have to overcome the habits of a lifetime. I know. I speak from experience. I'm an intense person with a very active mind. Leisure activities like bait fishing or croquet leave my mind free to return to the demands of the ministry. Hence, I must find a form of play that will engage my mind, at least initially, until I can shift gears.

Since, as we've already noted, one man's play is another man's work, it's important to establish simple criteria for distinguishing between work and play. Paul Thigpen says, "Real play, as opposed to work masquerading as play, is characterized by self-forgetfulness and an absorption in the activity at hand. Work concentrates on goals, achievements and turning out products. It's focused on the future. But play is centered on the present; on the joy of a process pleasurable in itself. When our 'play' becomes chiefly concerned with winning, keeping rules or reaching some 'educational' objective, it's no longer play. When the motivation is something besides fun, it's work."[2]

While pastoring in Craig, Colorado, I bought my first 35mm camera. It became my toy, my plaything. By Thigpen's definition my photography was play, not work, because it was characterized by self-forgetfulness and an absorption in the activity at hand. My only goal was the joy I derived from the act itself.

Creative photography is all-consuming. You have to give yourself to the process. It's a combination of art and discipline, intuition and technique. I've spent hours trailing deer through deep snow in order to get just the right shot. One winter morning, I awoke to a silent world wrapped in a fresh blanket of snow. Looking out the bedroom window, I noticed several wooden clothespins hanging on the clothesline. The wet snow was inches deep on them, creating a rare opportunity for a truly unusual photograph. Soon I was in the back yard, up to my knees in fresh snow, camera in hand. I spent the next two hours photographing close-ups of clothespins, snow-dusted winter weeds, and other unsightly paraphernalia made somehow comely by the season's first snow.

That morning's play continues to provide pleasure even now, almost ten years later. The series of clothespin pictures hangs in my secretary's office at the church and is a continual source of conversation.

The winter weeds are part of a collection in my study at home, and a snow-covered wagon wheel is included in the rustic decor of a country cabin owned by Brenda's parents. Let me make one thing clear: All of that is a consequence of play, a benefit, but definitely not the goal. When I ventured forth into the cold, camera in hand, I was not thinking of anything beyond the momentary pleasure of playing photographer. And I can truly say that the pleasure I derive from looking at the photographs now, from the many times I've discussed them with curious spectators, cannot come close to the joy I knew that winter morning when I played in the snow with my camera.

Many times I've been asked to photograph weddings and other special events. I suppose I really should feel complimented. I don't. Instead, I feel almost insulted. My play isn't for sale. Don't try to buy my hobby. Once I start accepting commissions, it becomes just another job. Occasionally, I have agreed to photograph special friends, but never for money. I do it for love — because I love them and I love taking pictures. If ever I start doing it for money I will have to find another hobby, because it won't be play anymore.

What am I trying to say? Simply this: Every one of us needs a hobby, a diversion. It doesn't really matter what we do as long as we do it with all our might and because we enjoy doing it. If accomplishments, productivity or financial remuneration are involved, it won't work. This is something we have to do just for the fun of it. Sir William Osler, the Canadian-born physician and distinguished professor of medicine at Johns Hopkins University, once told an audience of medical men: "No man is really happy or safe without a hobby, and it makes precious little difference what the outside interest may be — botany, beetles or butterflies; roses, tulips or irises; fishing, mountaineering or antiques — anything will do as long as he straddles a hobby and rides it hard."[3]

Chuck Swindoll's hobby, his camera as it were, is a radial arm saw, at least that's what he said in "A Cure For Tunnel Vision":

"The splinter in my thumb this morning brings back pleasant memories of yesterday's diversion. Cranking up the old radial arm saw in my garage, I wound up with two pecky cedar window box planters. I plunged into the project with the zeal of a paratrooper, ecstatic over the airborne sawdust, delighting over every angle, every nail, every hammer blow, even the feel of the wood and the scream of the saw. I caught myself thinking about nothing but the next cut . . . the exhilaration of accomplishment . . . the sheer joy of doing something totally opposite of my career and completely different from my calling.

"Periodically, I looked up through the sawdust and prayed, 'Lord, I sure do like doing this!' In this terror-filled aspirin age, my saw and I gave each other wide, toothy grins."[4]

I'm not really into woodworking but I have known a time or two when ". . . my saw and I gave each other wide, toothy grins."

A couple of years ago my brother and his family, who are missionaries in Argentina, were home on furlough, and we spent the better part of a week at Vallew. One evening we were sitting in front of the fireplace reliving our childhood when we decided to recreate it for our kids. Early the next morning we began building an elaborate tree house. For the next two days we hammered and sawed with a gusto that would have done Chuck Swindoll proud. We blistered our hands and bruised our thumbs, but it was well worth it. Not once did I think about my church or radio program, "Straight From the Heart." All my energies — mental, emotional and physical — were dedicated to that tree house. When we finished, we were tired and sore, but proud, and renewed in a way that only wholesome play can renew.

We celebrated our accomplishments with a cookout. Brenda and Melba (my sister-in-law) made chili over white-hot coals, and Don roasted huge knockwursts in true Argentine style. The kids were snugly ensconced in the tree house twenty feet overhead. For the rest of the afternoon we all were boys again, carefree, roaming the river bottom, doing our own version of Huck Finn. All good things must end, however, and the next morning we said our good-byes and went our separate ways. It was a week well spent. We had played hard, relived some old memories and made some new ones. Play had worked its magic again, and we returned to our work with renewed enthusiasm.

If photography, woodworking and the construction of tree houses leaves you cold, don't despair. There are hundreds of ways to play. In fact, the people who play best are those who have a variety of diversions. In addition to photography, my repertoire includes snowmobiling, deer hunting, basketball, racquetball and fishing. As I've already said, bait fishing is too slow for me, leaves my mind too free, and, believe you me, when my mind is left to its own ends, it always returns to the work of the ministry. However, spincasting for trout in a crystal-clear, ice-cold mountain stream is fishing of an altogether different genre.

First, you are always active, wading the river, never staying in one place. And you had better stay on your toes. One false step and you can get baptized in truly fundamental fashion. Then there's the constantly changing panorama of scenery — a hay meadow in the river bottom, a towering rock wall reflecting the subtle shades of the setting sun, a startled doe, water dripping from her wet muzzle, frozen for an instant before she bursts into graceful flight. The therapeutic exercise of casting requires enough concentration to keep the mind from wandering, but not enough to be mentally taxing. On a lazy, sunlit afternoon, it can be almost hypnotic — cast and retrieve, cast and retrieve . . . over and over again. With each cast, it seems the tension of life on the fast track lessens its hold. If you happen to get a strike, and generally you do, it provides just the right touch of exhilaration.

This kind of fishing also affords a unique combination of camaraderie and solitude. If you're fishing with a friend, there's the special joy of sharing a meaningful experience. Yet you are usually fishing several yards apart and the roar of the river makes conversation inconvenient at best and, often, downright impossible. You're together without really being together and, by the same token, you have solitude without really being alone. In short, you have the best of both worlds.

Shortly after we moved to Craig, Colorado, Brenda's mom and dad came to visit us. It was early September with just a hint of fall in the air, the perfect time to introduce a South Texan to the joys of trout fishing. I outfitted him with waders, a canvas creel, a fishing hat and a light rod. Soon we were nearly waist deep in the swiftly moving water of the William's Fork River. It was a good day for fishing, and we had our limit in almost no time. Still, the thing that stands out in my mind are the tomatoes.

Pastoring a small country church doesn't afford many perks, but one all metropolitan pastors might envy is the farm-fresh produce harvesttime provides. Just that morning a generous parishioner had delivered a big box of large, field-ripened tomatoes. Now, if all you've ever known are the plastic-like tomatoes you find in the supermarket, you probably won't be able to fully appreciate this experience. But if you've ever had a vine-ripe tomato, you'll know what I'm talking about. Anyway, let me get back to my story.

As we were leaving to go fishing, Brenda gave me a plastic bag with a half dozen of those big red hunkers. When we got to the river, I found a sheltered spot and submerged them so they would be good and cold when we got hungry. Now, it doesn't get hot in the Rockies like it does in South Texas, but by the time we got back to where we had left the tomatoes we were hot enough and more than a little sunburned. Retrieving the plastic bag, I handed Ben a tomato and took one for myself. Believe me, it's impossible to eat one of those babies without making a mess, but one nice thing about fishing is that you don't have to be too concerned about messes. I took a big bite, and my taste buds exploded. Tomato juice sprinkled with little yellow seeds ran down my chin. I looked over at Ben who was enjoying the same messy pleasure. We both grinned, realizing intuitively that life doesn't get any better than that.

Another time my dad and I were hunting deer, playing together, if you please. It was the last day of the season and I still hadn't filled my tag. At about eight o'clock in the morning we were easing the four-wheel drive pick-up along a cow trail when I slammed on the brakes and jumped out. I levered a shell into the chamber of my rifle and took aim on a clump of bushes about two hundred yards up the hill. I drew a breath, held it for just a moment and squeezed off my shot. Jumping back in the pick-up I cried, "I got him! A big one!" By now we were halfway up the hillside and bouncing around in the cab like a couple of crazy kids. Dad kept saying, "I didn't even see him."

At last we lurched to a stop and climbed out. Dad drew his hunting knife to field dress my buck. Only then did I tell him that I hadn't seen anything either. That I had just shot the hillside. At first he didn't laugh, in fact he was just a little peeved, but I was laughing so hard that he soon joined in. It wasn't the most exciting hunt I ever had, but I never had more fun, and that's what it's really all about.

By this time you may be tempted to ask what all of this "foolishness" has to do with living the spiritual life. A good enough question, and one which really underscores our need to return to a biblical theology of play. It seems that in our zeal to be conscientious, we have lost sight of the part play has in the whole scheme of life. We'll deal with this in detail in the next chapter, when we discuss the benefits of play, but for now let it suffice to say, "A cheerful heart is good medicine . . ." (Prov. 17:22).

It may also be helpful to remember that some of the giants of the Christian faith were playful men, men with a real sense of humor. For instance, several of Martin Luther's biographers picture him, not as a stern-faced reformer, but as a winsome, caring man. That is not to say that he couldn't be firm or even demanding and difficult at times, but that he knew the joy of living. It was this love for life that made him so appealing to the German people of his day.

Then there's Charles Spurgeon, that prince of English preachers. He was a character. In fact, his style was so fun-loving that he was criticized again and again for bordering on frivolity in the tabernacle pulpit. Once he replied, when some of his fellow clergymen took him to task for the humor in his sermons: "If only you knew how much I hold back, you would commend me . . . This preacher thinks it less a crime to cause a momentary laughter than a half-hour of profound slumber."[5] Now that's my kind of preacher!

Just this past week I was privileged to be one of the speakers at a special camp in Kansas. The evening speaker was Gene Jackson from Memphis, Tennessee. He was a riot. He described his homiletical style as "kick the can" — give it a good whack and go after it. In truth, his sermons were scripturally sound and well thought-out. And it was his humor, his ability to poke fun at himself and us, which made some of his most telling points bearable. Sometimes, life is so painful that if we couldn't laugh, I don't think we could bear it. And one of God's best gifts is a preacher with the ability to make us laugh without letting us off the hook. Jackson did that as well as anyone I've ever heard, and I'm in his debt.

He told of taking his blind daughter to school one miserable morning in mid-January. The temperature was just above freezing and a light drizzle made driving treacherous. He was in a foul mood when he finally sat down at the counter in his favorite donut shop for a cup of coffee before going to the office. He was trying to warm his stiff hands over the steaming coffee when the guy next to him asked, "How are you doing?" Jackson replied, "I'm wet and cold and sick to death of fighting traffic. Every little old lady in Memphis must be on the streets this morning."

Well, the guy didn't know when to leave well enough alone and he plunged ahead, "You're having a tough day, huh?" Jackson grunted a reply, "You might say that."

The guy wouldn't quit. "I used to have days like that before I made Jesus my savior. Now He gives me joy even on my bad days."

By now Jackson was feeling a little guilty, but he didn't want anyone messing up his depression, so he just grunted in an unfriendly sort of way. Undeterred, the guy persisted. "What kind of business are you in?"

Now that's the last thing a minister wants to talk about, given the circumstances, so Jackson said rather abruptly, "I don't want to talk about it." Then he really felt guilty and relented. He told the guy he was a preacher, and they both had a good laugh. That's the sort of humor that makes life bearable, and it's the stuff real play is made of.

If things have been a little rough lately, if you've been short with your spouse or your children, perhaps you need a good side-splitting laugh. Why don't you take a minute and think of some of the really funny things that have happened to you over the years. Or maybe you ought to do something really crazy like wear a gorilla mask to the dinner table. Lighten up a little bit. Don't take yourself so seriously. Fun and games are a part of life too, you know!

Footnotes

1. Charles R. Swindoll, *Growing Strong In The Seasons Of Life* (Portland: Multnomah Press, 1983), p. 100.

2. Paul Thigpen, "Dad, Are We Having Fun Yet?" *Charisma*, June 1987, p. 46.

3. Sir William Osler, *Familiar Quotations,* ed. John Bartlett (Boston: Little, Brown and Company, 1955).

4. Swindoll, p. 119.

5. J. Oswald Sanders, *Spiritual Leadership* (Chicago: Moody Press, 1967), pp. 59,60.

Chapter 11

THE BENEFITS OF PLAY

This is a dangerous chapter. Not because play has no benefits, but because focusing on the benefits tends to turn play into another form of work. Or, as Paul Thigpen says, "When our 'play' becomes chiefly concerned with winning, keeping rules or reaching some 'educational' objective, it's no longer play. When the motivation is something besides fun, it's work."[1] For play to be play, it must have no goal but play itself.

Why then do I even raise the issue? Because, as I've already said, nothing kills play faster than a guilty conscience, and for the most part, we are all products of the work ethic which says play is pretty pointless. For people with that mind-set, playing is a waste, and such frivolity, grounds for feeling guilty. In order to play well, we must overcome this conditioning. We can do this in at least two ways. First, by realizing that God wills our play, that He designed it as an intrinsic part of the rhythm of life, that there is a time, a season, to laugh and play! Second, by recognizing the inherent benefits of play.

Here's the danger: If we play in order to derive the benefits, then it's not play anymore. Yet if we don't acknowledge the benefits, we may not be able to overcome either our propensity for work or our lingering guilt. Maybe we can best negotiate these difficult waters by differentiating between goals and consequences, and by keeping that distinction clearly before us. Play's only goal is playing, having fun! Whatever benefits we derive from our play — a lessening of stress, physical exercise, enhanced parent/child relationships, etc. — are nothing more than a consequence. Against that backdrop, let's turn our attention to the benefits of play.

Recreational play (athletic games, hunting, fishing and other outdoor sports like skiing, etc.), especially play which involves vigorous physical exercise, is particularly good for reducing stress, the bane of modern life, and for improving overall physical conditioning. Dr. Gary Collins calls exercise "nature's tranquilizer." He writes:

"Studies have shown that when people exercise regularly they feel better, sleep more soundly, handle problems better, and are more able to cope with life. Exercise on a regular basis is good for the body, and this in turn can reduce anxiety and inoculate us so that we can better handle future stresses.

"For people who enjoy sports, such activities as handball, swimming, golf, or tennis can be good stress-reducers provided they are done regularly, are not overly strenuous, and are not played with such keen competition that more stress is aroused. For others, daily jogging or calisthenics can keep us from getting too flabby or tense."[2]

Let me share a case in point. For the past seven or eight years, I have suffered repeatedly from atypical migraine headaches. As a general rule, I had one about once a week but during especially stressful times I might have two or three in a week's time. I saw several doctors and experimented with a variety of treatments, but nothing really seemed to help. In addition, I suffered from muscle spasms in my neck and shoulders, causing me no little discomfort. By monitoring these painful episodes, I was able to determine that they appeared to be stress related.

On February 24, 1983, I wrote in my journal: "Lord, yesterday was horrible. I awoke with a headache and it continued to get worse until I was forced to go home to bed at 1:30 P.M. Yet it was a good day also. Last night I started reading *Nurturing Silence In A Noisy Heart*. As I read, I discovered that my headaches are a cry for privacy, solitude. In my normal schedule, Monday and Saturday are my private days. I can give of myself almost totally the other five days if I seclude myself Monday and Saturday. I need two days out of seven to be alone, away from the demanding crowd.

"Mondays are for Brenda and me. Coffee and the morning paper. Books and naps. Closeness and conversation. Saturdays are for time alone with the Word in preparation for Sunday.

"Sometimes it's not possible. Board retreats, company for the weekend. Still, when that happens, I must take another day for myself, at least one day to be alone. Help me, Lord, to do it faithfully.

"Thank You for a wife and daughter who do not demand what I don't have to give. And thank You for allowing me the freedom to live within my limits. Amen."

By honoring this discovery I was able to control my headaches, but not eliminate them. Just as sure as I got caught up in the rush of life and missed my day off or allowed people and events to crowd into my Saturdays, I would experience several headaches with a vengeance!

This went on for about three years; then I decided to add recreational play to my work/rest routine. To be absolutely honest, it didn't start out as play at all, but as a workout. I was twenty pounds overweight, terribly out of shape and under a lot of stress. Past experience had taught me that I lacked the discipline to maintain a vigorous exercise program such as aerobics or jogging, so I decided on racquetball. I knew that I would have to fool my body into thinking it was having fun if I ever hoped to exercise consistently.

An amazing thing happened — my exercise turned into play! I found that I loved racquetball. I started playing because I needed the exercise, but soon I was playing just for the fun of it. For sixty sweaty minutes I thought of nothing but serves and kill shots. I wasn't trying to get in shape, lose weight or reduce stress. I was there to play. I was having fun! Winning wasn't important, and a good thing, too, because for the first three or four months everyone beat me like a drum. Still, morning after morning, I would walk off the court at eight o'clock absolutely exhilarated, soaked with sweat and gasping for breath.

In less than a month I noticed that my headaches were decreasing. After about ninety days they had virtually disappeared. There were other things which also indicated a reduction in stress, but none was as dramatic as what was happening with my headaches. The key for me was a regular Sabbath (Monday), a day of solitude to prepare for Sunday, and lots of vigorous physical exercise on the racquetball court at least three times a week. Let me violate that rhythm, and it's just a matter of days until the headaches return.

Since stress is a significant factor in our general health, especially in heart disease, I have undoubtedly improved my overall health and increased my life expectancy. That's not why I play racquetball, but it is a nice bonus! In addition, I have lost twenty pounds and had the opportunity to develop several new relationships. Who says play doesn't pay? Besides, I'm having a blast!

An added benefit of recreational play is the opportunity to develop meaningful relationships. There's a sense of camaraderie when you huddle together in a duck blind in the predawn darkness, swap fish stories over coffee, or relive the big play in the bottom of the ninth. Many a lifelong friendship has been forged on the field of play.

While we're on the subject of relationships, let's talk about the benefits of family play. Did you hear about the father in Montgomery, Alabama, who really loved his family and wanted them to have a memorable vacation? The press of business kept him tied to the office, but he insisted that they go without him. They didn't want to. In fact, they argued that they wouldn't, but, in the end, Dad prevailed.

"He helped them plan every day of the camping trip. They would load up the family station wagon, drive to California, camp up and down the coast, then travel back home together. Each day was carefully arranged — even the highways they would travel and the places they would stop. Dad knew their whole route, the time they would reach each state — planned almost to the hour — even when they would cross the Great Divide.

"It's what he didn't tell them that made the difference.

"The father took off work (he'd planned it all along) and arranged to have himself flown to an airport near where his family would be on that particular day of the trip. He had also arranged to have someone pick him up and drive him to a place where every car on that route had to pass. With a wide grin, he sat on his sleeping bag and waited for the arrival of that familiar station wagon packed full of kids and camping gear. When he spotted the station wagon, he stood up, stepped out onto the shoulder of the road and stuck out his thumb.

"Can you visualize it?

" 'Look! That guy looks just like . . . DAD!'

"The family assumed he was a thousand miles away, sweating over a stack of papers. It's amazing they didn't drive off into a ditch or collapse from heart failure. Can you imagine the fun they had the rest of the way? And the memories they stored away in their mental scrapbook — could they ever be forgotten?

"When later asked why he would go to all that trouble, the creative father replied, 'Well . . . someday I'm going to be dead. When that happens, I want my kids and wife to say, "You know, Dad was a lot of fun." ' "[3]

167

Families who play together do have lots of fun! They make memories which will enrich their lives and the lives of their children and even their grandchildren for a lifetime. They're building relationships which will last. My dad was more pedestrian than the aforementioned father but no less dedicated to the happiness and well-being of his family. Somehow, year after year, he managed to take us on vacations he couldn't afford, in order to make memories we couldn't afford to be without. Still, it was some of the more spontaneous things we shared which stand out in my mind these many years later.

I remember a Christmas Eve when I was about ten or eleven. We hadn't received any snow that winter and it was unseasonably warm, not the kind of Christmas a kid hopes for. We'll take a white Christmas every time, the whiter the better.

It was traditional in our family to open our gifts on Christmas Eve, after supper, making the twenty-fourth of December at least twice as long as any other day of the year. On this particular day, Dad got off work at noon and decided to take Mom and us three boys to the sand pits east of town. Dad, Don and I spent the afternoon leaping off the high bluffs to land twenty feet below in the deep sand. Then we'd climb the bluff again, take a good run to build up speed, and leap out into space, screaming like Comanche Indians on the warpath. We did it again and again, all afternoon long, while Mother sat in the car and tended our baby brother, Bob. I don't even remember what I got for Christmas that year, but I've never forgotten playing in the sand pits with Dad!

We did a lot of other things together as a family, as well. I can remember going to Chimney Canyons as a small boy, probably before I was five years old. I watched Dad and Uncle Denny target shoot with their .22 rifles. They always let us kids have the brass cartridges from the spent ammo. Somehow, I thought it was the bullet itself and, for the life of me, I couldn't figure out how they could get to the bottom of the canyon and retrieve it without being seen. Each time they handed me a shell I would tell myself not to watch the target but to keep my eyes on Dad. Still, my attention would be irresistibly drawn to the target, and once more I would be left holding a brass cartridge and puzzling over the unsolved mystery. No one else seemed to find it puzzling, so I kept my confusion to myself. In fact, this may be the first time I've shared it with anyone.

There were four of us kids. I'm the oldest, then there's Don and Bob and, finally, our "baby" sister, Sherry. When we all get together for the holidays and start reminiscing, it's a riot. Our memories are different, the things that stand out in our minds are highly personalized, but the one consistency is that we all have our share. Perhaps this one thing, more than anything else, is proof of the value of family play. It not only makes for good memories, but for good people.

Arthur Gordon reminds us of this when he writes:

"Children are naturally inquisitive and love to try new things. But they cannot find these things by themselves; someone must offer them the choices. Years ago, when the Quiz Kids were astonishing American radio audiences with their brilliance, a writer set out to discover what common denominators there were in the backgrounds of these extraordinary children. He found that some were from poor families, some from rich; some had been to superior schools, some had not.

"But, in every case investigated, there was one parent, sometimes two, who shared enthusiasms with the child, who watched for areas of interest, who gave encouragement and praise for achievement, who made a game of searching out the answers to questions, who went out of his way to supply the tools of learning. No doubt the capacity for outstanding performance was already there, but it took the love and interest and companionship of a parent to bring it out."[4]

Leah, our daughter, is seventeen now, and a lot of our play and memory-making is behind us. The things she remembers are probably different from those her mother and I recall, and that's as it should be. I remember watching Brenda play "Hobbie" with

Leah when she was not yet two. A "Hobbie" is a make-believe tickle bug that loves to tickle little kids. It's a carry-over from Brenda's childhood, and we entertained ourselves and Leah for hours with it. Brenda would hold her open hand at arm's length above Leah, who was lying on her back, and begin a tantalizing descent toward her bare tummy. Before Brenda could ever touch her, Leah would burst into happy giggles. She never got enough of the "Hobbie" and would always cry, "More, Mommy, more."

My contribution was the "Mad Duck Game." It was something I made up. In the middle of a sentence, I would suddenly start quacking deep in my throat. The only way I could stop was for Leah to hit me on the back and knock that mad duck right out of my throat. It sounds silly as I write it. It probably was silly, but we had loads of fun with it.

What am I trying to say? Simply this: What we play and how we play is not nearly as important as the fact that we play. It's not the game so much as it is the time and fun we give to our children. It's the raw material of which our later relationships are made. I'm convinced that juvenile delinquency begins in early childhood, although it seldom manifests itself before the early teen years. When a child becomes a teenager, he is finally old enough to act out his anger. If you want to enjoy your children when they are teenagers, play with them every day of their lives! Remember, the family that truly plays together stays together.

As Leah grew older, our play changed. Brenda taught her to ride a bike and roller-skate. I taught her backgammon and chess. The first time we took her fishing, she caught a four-and-one-half pound salmon out of a secluded lake high in the Rockies, near the Wyoming border. She was barely six, and after several minutes she asked me to take her spinning rod, saying, "Help me, Daddy. I'm tired." We ice-skated together, rode snowmobiles, picnicked on Rabbit Ears Pass, and vacationed from Argentina to Mexico City to Canada and several places in between, playing all the way. We never had much money to spend, but that only made us more resourceful, more creative. I only hope Leah remembers her childhood with the same fondness that I remember mine.

Remember, play comes in a lot of different packages. It doesn't have to be games or contests or anything, for that matter. It's simply two or more people enjoying life just for the fun of it. The fact that their play may enhance their relationship is incidental. The fact that they are making memories and establishing family rituals doesn't enter their minds, either. That will come later, years later. For now it's just fun and games, just play.

By now, you've probably concluded that Arthur Gordon is one of my favorite writers. You're right, so let me quote him again:

"One summer night in a seaside cottage, a small boy felt himself lifted from bed. Dazed with sleep, he heard his mother murmur about the lateness of the hour, heard his father laugh. Then he was borne in his father's arms, with the swiftness of a dream, down the porch steps, out onto the beach.

"Overhead the sky blazed with stars. 'Watch!' his father said. And incredibly, as he spoke, one of the stars moved. In a streak of golden fire, it flashed across the astonished heavens. And before the wonder of this could fade, another star leaped from its place, and then another, plunging toward the restless sea. 'What is it?' the child whispered. 'Shooting stars,' his father said. 'They come every year on certain nights in August. I thought you'd like to see the show.'

"That was all: just an unexpected glimpse of something haunting and mysterious and beautiful. But, back in bed, the child stared for a long time into the dark, rapt with the knowledge that all around the quiet house the night was full of the silent music of the falling stars.

"Decades have passed, but I remember that night still, because I was the fortunate seven-year-old whose father believed that a new experience was more important for a small boy than an unbroken night's sleep. No doubt in my childhood I had the usual quota of playthings, but these are forgotten now. What I remember is the night the stars fell, the day we rode in a caboose, the time we tried to skin the alligator, the telegraph we made that really worked.

171

I remember the trophy table in the hall where we children were encouraged to exhibit things we had found — snakeskins, seashells, flowers, arrowheads — anything unusual or beautiful.

". . . Many years have passed since that night in my life when the stars fell, but the earth still turns, the sun still sets, night still sweeps over the changeless sea. And next year when August comes with its shooting stars, my son will be seven."[5]

In addition to family play or parent/child play, there is also marital play. Its benefits include conflict resolution, better communications and enhanced intimacy. R. William Betcher, a Massachusetts clinical psychologist, has been doing research for five years on the contribution of spontaneous play to marital adjustment:

"He found that the common factor in intimate play of all kinds is its ability to stabilize a relationship; it seems to help couples keep a balance between too much distance, which of course alienates them from each other, and too much intimacy, which is apt to be threatening.

"Besides this general function, Betcher found that play fills very specific needs. It can serve as an end run around sensitive spots; it can be a way of saying potentially hurtful things — voicing criticism, for instance, or expressing wishes that could destroy a marriage if they were actually realized — without hurting anyone. Play is thus a means of defusing conflict. It is also one of the best ways to probe someone's intimate thoughts and feelings, and therefore serves to draw partners together and to cement the bonds between them."[6]

One of the first benefits of spontaneous marital play is that it defuses family conflict. Dick Foth, who is the president of Bethany Bible College, relates a personal incident which illustrates this benefit well.

As president of the college, he is required to be deeply involved in fund-raising, which necessitates a considerable amount of travel.

Some time ago, he returned from a particularly demanding trip to find the house littered with the children's toys and other things. Grumpily he complained, "Why is the house always such a mess?"

If you've been married for any length of time, you undoubtedly recognize that as a potentially volatile situation. Here's a lady who, week after week, finds herself being both mother and father to four kids while their daddy is flying all over the country raising money for the college. Mothering four children is a big job even if the husband is around to help. When he's gone a lot, it can be absolutely exhausting.

It reminds me of the woman who boarded a city bus with seven rambunctious youngsters and collapsed on the nearest seat. Her hair was a mess, there were large black circles under her eyes, and weariness clung to her like fine dust. As she stumbled toward the exit at her stop, her wiggling tribe trailing behind, a fellow passenger asked, "Do all these children belong to you, or is this some kind of picnic?"

She looked at that man through squinted eyes and said, "They're all mine, mister, and believe me, it's no picnic!"

Well, rearing four children, mostly by yourself is no picnic either, and who could blame Mrs. Foth if she had responded angrily. She didn't. Instead, she said, "Children, please pick up your things, the President is home." She said it with a smile and everyone laughed, but Dick got the message, loud and clear.

Charlie Shedd, in his insightful book *Letters To Phillip: On How To Treat A Woman*, quotes a happy wife whose husband had the knack of using playful comments to make important points. She said: "Once in a while Tommy sticks his chest out and says, 'Now listen to me, squaw! Get back in your wigwam. I'm the chief and don't you forget it!' "

"On first hearing," Shedd adds, "you might think this borders on rough handling. But this is what she says:

" 'It's funny what this does. When he says it nice, I get the best feeling. You know, all secure . . .!' "[7]

173

The key here is "When he says it nice . . ." We are not talking about sarcasm, or cruelty disguised as humor. This is genuine play, loving play, used to defuse conflict.

When I do premarital counseling, I usually ask the couple if they have any private rituals, shared jokes or personal nicknames that have special meaning just to them. Invariably they become embarrassed. I hasten to inform them that it's not just silliness but a vital ingredient in all healthy marriages. K.C. Cole, reporting in *Psychology Today*, writes:

"All happy couples aren't alike, so there is no single litmus test for a good marriage. But if one studies couples systematically over time, it becomes apparent that many of them share a characteristic that signals, more often than not, a healthy union. It's nothing so obvious as a satisfying sexual relationship, or shared interests, or the habit of talking out disputes freely. It is, rather, a capacity for playfulness of a kind that transcends fun and reflects considerably more than the partners' ability to amuse each other. Private nicknames, shared jokes and fantasies, mock insults, make-believe fighting — all these might seem like mere silliness. In fact, they may stand in for, or lubricate, more complex transactions, essential but potentially painful or even destructive."[8]

I know a couple who use play regularly as a way to initiate communication. When he wants to know what's going on in her world, he pretends to be a gossipy old woman. With a sly grin, he says, "The old woman in me wants to know if you have any good gossip to share." Then he pretends to be leaning over the back fence while she proceeds to talk about what's happening in her life. If circumstances conspire to trap them in busyness, and communication is neglected for a few days, he sometimes says things like, "The old gossip in me thinks you don't like her anymore." Or, "Let's meet over the back fence and swap gossip." Silly? Perhaps, but I don't really think so. Isn't that better than, "You never talk to me!"?

Spontaneous marital play can also enhance intimacy. A scene from the novel *Michael* by G. Robert James is a good example.

It is early evening. Michael, a writer, has just finished his day's work when Patricia, his wife, enters with two steaming mugs of spiced tea. Seated in front of a window, which opens on a mountain meadow, they share the tea and the quietness as evening introduces the night. After a bit, Michael plants a kiss on the end of her nose and asks, ". . . Have I told you today how pretty you are?"

"Oh, Michael, you're silly!" she responds, her pleasure obvious. "I'm seven-and-a-half months pregnant and huge. I can't even walk anymore, I just sort of waddle."

"Well," he said appraising her critically, "now that you mention it your figure does seem a little lumpy."

"You're nothing but a dirty old man," she accuses him feigning anger. "I'm heavy with your child and now you don't want anything more to do with me."

"That's where you're wrong, ma'am," he teased, giving her a lecherous look. "I'm fiendishly interested in women who are seven-and-a-half months pregnant and waddle."

"You fool," she said affectionately as she hoisted herself out of the chair and moved toward the door. "I'll prepare dinner."[9]

Given that kind of tender play, it's not hard to imagine a couple capable of sharing intimacy on all levels — spiritually, emotionally and sexually. Besides, it must be fun to share those witticisms and act out those roles. Lest you think such behavior not fitting for the people of God, let me remind you of Isaac and Rebekah's behavior described in Genesis 26:8:

"And it came to pass, when he had been there a long time, that Abimelech king of the Philistines looked out at a window, and saw, and, behold, Isaac was sporting with Rebekah his wife" (KJV).

The Hebrew word for "sporting" literally means to laugh out loud, to play or make sport. Given the context, we can only conclude that Isaac was flirting with Rebekah, participating in some form of love play with her.

Let's close this chapter with a quick review. First, there are different kinds of play, and they each have their own benefits. Recreational play is just that — ball games of all kinds, swimming and skiing, and, of course, fishing, hunting and camping. The primary benefits of recreational play are a reduction of stress and an improvement in your overall physical well-being. Family play or parent/child play involves games, picnics, vacations, and a host of other family activities where fun is king. This kind of play builds relationships and makes memories which often last a lifetime. The third and final kind of play we considered was marital play. Its chief benefits include conflict resolution, increased communications between husband and wife, and enhanced intimacy.

Remember, we must always guard against playing for the wrong reasons. If we look beyond the act of play itself to the benefits, then it's not play anymore but just another form of work. The benefits of play must always be a consequence and not a goal, something that happens but not something we seek. Play's only goal is play itself, and it is its own reward!

Footnotes

1. Thigpen, p. 46.

2. Dr. Gary Collins, *You Can Profit From Stress* (Santa Ana: Vision House Publishers, 1977), pp. 208,209.

3. Bruce Larson, "The One And Only You," *Growing Strong In The Seasons Of Life* by Charles Swindoll (Portland: Multnomah Press, 1983), p. 211.

4. Gordon, pp. 152,153.

5. Ibid., pp. 150,151,154.

6. K.C. Cole, "Playing Together: From Couples That Play," *Psychology Today*, Feb. 1982.

7. Charlie W. Shedd, *Letters To Phillip: On How To Treat A Woman* (Garden City: Doubleday & Company, Inc., 1968), p. 2.

8. Cole.

9. James, pp. 288,289.

Chapter 12

MAKING PLAY A PRIORITY

For the past two chapters we've been talking about play. Now I want us to focus on time, time management to be exact, and how it affects our play. Over the years, I've picked up some homespun wisdom which has helped me enormously in this area. Someone, I can't remember who, said, "You always have time for what you do first." Most people who don't play claim to be too busy, claim they just don't have the time. The truth of the matter is, they have the same amount of time as the rest of us, but they have chosen to spend it on something other than play. Which brings me to the second bit of wisdom. My friend and fellow pastor, Allen Groff, frequently says, "We don't need more books to tell us how to manage our time, that's not the problem. We need to learn to manage ourselves!"

Our problem is twofold. Ignorance — we know almost nothing about the rhythm of life which is intrinsically woven into the whole of nature. Motivation — without understanding we tend to distort the values of work, rest, worship and play, which results in confused and misplaced motivation.

According to Gordon Dahl:

"Most middle-class Americans tend to worship their work, to work at their play, and to play at their worship. As a result, their meanings and values are distorted. Their relationships disintegrate faster than they can keep them in repair, and their lifestyles resemble a cast of characters in search of a plot."[1]

Let's address these areas one at a time. First, the rhythm of life. The Scriptures repeatedly allude to this principle:

" 'As long as the earth endures,
seedtime and harvest,
cold and heat,
summer and winter,
day and night
will never cease.' "
Genesis 8:22

"There is a time for everything,
and a season for every activity
under heaven."
Ecclesiastes 3:1

". . . The race is not to the swift
or the battle to the strong,
nor does food come to the wise
or wealth to the brilliant
or favor to the learned;
but time and chance happen to them
all."
Ecclesiastes 9:11

The Sabbath itself, which consecrated every seventh day as a day of rest and worship, holy unto the Lord, was just a reflection of this principle, an affirmation of the rhythm of life. The Lord further emphasizes this rhythm by instituting a sabbath year.

Leviticus 25:1-5 declares:

"The Lord said to Moses on Mount Sinai, 'Speak to the Israelites and say to them: "When you enter the land I am going to give you, the land itself must observe a sabbath to the Lord. For six years sow your fields, and for six years prune your vineyards and gather their crops. But in the seventh year the land is to have a sabbath of rest, a sabbath to the Lord. Do not sow your fields or prune your vineyards. Do not reap what grows of itself or harvest the grapes of your untended vines. The land is to have a year of rest." ' "

In short, God is saying that life's richness, its fullness, flows out of its rhythm. God and man, land and beast, all creatures great and small, are so created that they can experience total fruition only by observing the rhythm of life. Only a madman would try to plant in the dead of winter or harvest in seedtime. The fruitfulness of his labors depend on his willingness to work within the seasons of nature, within the rhythm of the land. By the same token, we live self-defeating lives when we ignore the divinely ordained rhythm of work and rest, worship and play. It's counter-productive to work when we should be playing, and the sooner we busy-beaver types learn this, the better off we'll all be!

Many conscientious people contend that play is out of place in a world as needy as ours. Eloquently, they argue that play will have to wait. Life is too short, the need too great. To which I respond: "Surely God anticipated the enormity of human need, still He ordained the rhythm of life. In His infinite wisdom, He decreed that life should have a season for play." Don't misunderstand me. I'm not an insensitive, uncaring man, urging you to fiddle while Rome burns. To the contrary. I, too, have to overcome my need-centered theology in order to practice the rhythm of life, especially to play. A recent entry in my journal will give you an idea of my own struggles.

"Lord,
help me. I feel overwhelmed.
The needs of our broken world
far exceed my limited resources
of both time and money.

179

"Day after day I receive new requests —
a missionary pleads for monthly support,
so he can leave for his appointed field.
The National Christian Women's Movement requests
funds to fight court cases across the country.
The International Prison Fellowship is planning
a nationwide prison invasion.
They need manpower and money.

"There's more, lots more —
the Crisis Pregnancy Ministry needs more
host families.
A minister dies of cancer, leaving his widow
hospital bills totaling thousands of dollars.
Memorial Day weekend is the annual Aged
Ministers Assistance Day offering.
Oral Roberts Evangelistic Association wants
help in scholarshipping medical students for the
healing teams.
The revival in Argentina needs funds
for tents and buildings to conserve the harvest.
The General Council requests a special offering
to offset a $500,000 deficit in administrative
expenses.

"The list goes on and on . . .

"The Scriptures are little help:
We are instructed to feed the hungry,
care for the widows and the fatherless,
visit those who are in prison,
and take the Gospel to the ends of the world.

"How do we decide where to invest
our limited resources of time and money?
It seems no matter what I do it's not enough.
Try as I may, it seems I always
end up feeling I should do more,
give more . . .

"Help me, Lord,
   I don't know what to do!"

* *

My Child,
Seek My counsel and I will direct you.
Give what you have and leave the rest to Me.
I will take your gifts and make them enough,
even as I used the five loaves and two fishes
to feed the thousands.
When you've done your best,
there is no reason to feel guilty.
Compassion, yes, but not condemnation,
   never condemnation!
The work is Mine, not yours.
I am the Lord of harvest.

* *

What does all of this mean? Just this: We must live God-centered, God-directed lives, not need-centered lives. Compassion born only out of sympathy for suffering humanity risks both the extremes of fanaticism and burnout. Healing compassion, on the other hand, combines the love and guidance of the Creator with a genuine concern for the hurting in our world. If our only motivation is need, we will be swallowed up, we will risk becoming part of the problem rather than part of the solution. Our only hope is to let God define our area of responsibility and then to live within our limits, both emotionally and physically. It's not easy to do, but it's the only hope we have. The alternatives — all-consuming fanaticism or self-centered apathy — are not alternatives at all.

It's time we came to grips with the facts of life. As Jesus said, " 'You will always have the poor among you . . .' " (John 12:8). That's not an excuse for doing nothing; it's just the harsh reality of the human condition. The truth is, no matter how sacrificially we live, no matter how much we give, we will never eradicate the tragedy of human misery. There's a certain danger in acknowledging as much, for there will always be those insensitive souls who will use it as an argument for doing nothing, which is a gross denial of the Gospel Jesus taught. The fact is, we all have certain responsibilities, God-given patches of humanity, as it were, to love, and nothing can absolve us of that.

Norman Cousins addresses this issue forthrightly when he writes:

"Compassion is not quantitative. Certainly it is true that behind every human being who cries out for help there may be a million or more equally entitled to attention. But this is the poorest of all reasons for not helping the person whose cries you hear . . . Reach out and take hold of the one who happens to be nearest. If you are never able to help or save another, at least you will have saved one. To help put meaning into a single life may not produce universal regeneration, but it happens to represent the basic form of energy in a society. It also is the test of individual responsibility."[2]

And even as we come to grips with the fact that we can't change the whole world, that there will always be open sores and crying needs, we must also realize that in the midst of all of that we must also choose to play; to laugh and cry with those we love best. Without that, our most important relationships will wither and die.

"Celebrate the temporary,
Don't wait until tomorrow,
Live today.
Celebrate the simple things.
Enjoy the butterfly.
Embrace the snow.
Run with the ocean.
Delight in the trees.

"Or a single lonely flower.

"Go barefoot in the wet grass.

"Don't wait
Until all the problems are solved,
Or all the bills are paid.

"You will wait forever.
Eternity will come and go,
And you
Will still be waiting.

"Live in the now,
With all its problems and its agonies,
With its joy,
And its pain.

"Celebrate your pain,
Your despair,
Your anger.
It means you're alive.
Look closer,
Breathe deeper.
Stand taller.
Stop grieving the past.

"There is joy and beauty
Today.

"It is temporary,
Here now and gone.
So celebrate it
While you can.
Celebrate the temporary."[3]

Finding time to play has never been easy for me. Over the years, I've repeatedly allowed myself to become trapped in weeks, and sometimes even months, of grinding work. I can always tell when I need to take a break, though. My creative juices dry up, I become irritable, life loses its zest. Of late, though, I've made an interesting observation — the last place my exhaustion manifests itself is in my public ministry. I can remain effective long past the point at which I've ceased being personally fulfilled. If I act on this information quickly and restore rhythm to my life, renewal is just days away. Every day that I delay, however, edges me ever closer to burnout.

About four years ago, I was in the middle of one of those "grinding" periods. There were a number of extenuating factors — we had just added two new staff members, "Straight From The Heart" (our radio ministry) was just weeks old and requiring the kind of attention all newborns demand, and the church was undergoing some internal changes of its own. All in all, I just didn't see any way to take some time off. A perceptive, and I might add persistent, young couple picked up on the signs and invited me to bring my family and join them for a day's sailing. I declined as graciously as I could, pleading a mountain of work.

They were sympathetic but persistent, and creative, I might add! Knowing my susceptibility to anything either creative or romantic, they designed and mailed me a formal invitation requesting the honor of my presence for a Saturday of sailing. Well, that was too much for me. I accepted, howbeit somewhat reluctantly. Without question, that was one of the best decisions of my life. Not only did they introduce us to the joys of sailing, but it was the beginning of a very special friendship as well. I can't help wondering at the injustice I might have done myself if I hadn't made time to play.

Shortly after that, circumstances made it necessary for them to sell their sailboat, which just further illustrates the importance of playing when the opportunity presents itself. There will always be work, deadlines and demands. We can't afford to wait until we're "all caught up," or we'll never play. Remember, many of life's richest experiences are birthed in the moment of play, among them friendships that last a lifetime.

I think it was Arthur Gordon who related an experience from his childhood, which might well become a model for us all. It was summertime and the circus was in town for its annual visit. As far as he and his brother were concerned, it was the highlight of the summer. They couldn't wait for Saturday afternoon to come. Just as they were stepping out the door with their father, the phone rang. Their hearts dropped when their mother said their dad's boss was on the line. It wasn't unusual for him to be called back to work, and they braced themselves, as best they could, for the inevitable disappointment. To their amazement, they heard their dad say, "I'm sorry, but I've promised to take the boys to the circus and I can't disappoint them." There was more, in the same vein, but they had heard all they needed to hear.

It must have been a difficult conversation, because when their dad finally hung up they heard their mother say, "If you really need to go in, go on. I'm sure the boys will understand. After all, the circus will be back next year." With sensitivity and insightful wisdom, their father responded, "Yes, but childhood won't. You're young only once."

How different from the father Joseph Donders describes in "The Tired Samaritan":

"I knew a family
far from here
who had a father
who really lived the story of
that Samaritan.

"He was always busy;
he was always helping others;
he was a member of all kinds
of organizations
trying to improve
the lot of suffering humankind;
he really had made a
    100 percent option
for the poor.

"But because of that
he had never any time
for his wife;
he never had any time
to sit down with his children;
he was always busy
day and night
with the ones
alongside the road.
   One day his daughter of fourteen
   wanted to talk to him
   about something very important,
   but every time she asked her father
   to listen to her,
   her father
   had no time to sit down;
   he was busy,
   again and again.
She went to her mother
asking her what to do,
and her mother said:
'Undo your hair,
put some dirt on your face,
dress in some rags,
walk barefoot,
and knock at his office door,
and you will see that he will
   receive you
and listen
because he will consider you
to be a stranger.'
   That is what she did.
   Her father, of course,
   recognized her immediately,
   but he understood
   and sat down.

"Dag Hammarskjold,
who was for years the
    Secretary General
of the United Nations,
wrote in his diary:
    'People who are worried about
    the world issues,
    about global problems,
    very easily forget
    the smaller issues.
    If you are not willing to be good
    in the smaller circle
    of your family and friends,
    you can't do anything
    for humanity as such.
    Without that intimacy,
    you live in a world of abstractions,
    in which your solipsism,
    your hunger for power,
    your destructive tendencies,
    maim their only
        more powerful opponent:
    love.'
It is better to be good
with all one's heart
to one person
than to sacrifice
oneself
for the whole of humanity."[4]

A telling point, isn't it? Let's start by being good to our families, especially our children. It will take a disciplined commitment for most of us, because we've been taught to put away childish things like make-believe, curiosity, imagination, and play, especially play. We're into adult things like responsibility and work, busyness and work, religion and work. In fact, it seems work has gotten into every part of our lives. Kids, on the other hand, will only work if they think it's play. Remember how Tom Sawyer conned all his friends into helping him paint the fence? By pretending it was great fun.

Take off your tie, roll up your sleeves, get down on the floor, on your child's level, and play. Tomorrow he will be grown and gone. Believe me, I know. Just yesterday I was giving Leah piggyback rides and teaching her to fly a kite. Today I watch in stunned disbelief as she gets in her car and drives off to work her shift at the pizza restaurant. Allowing myself a moment of self-congratulation, I decide she's turned out pretty well. We must have done something right, her mother and I. Still, where have all the years gone? Now and then I can't help thinking how nice it would be if we could go back and play together again. Nothing planned, nothing really special, just spontaneous play — without rules or reasons, just for the fun of it!

"Lord,
kids are so neat!
Sometimes they're bundles of energy
gift wrapped in hand-me-downs.

"Other times they're
pajamaed packages of sleepy sweetness.
Always they're a miracle.

"I love the way they chase butterflies,
and the attention they give to mud puddles
and raindrops on a window.

"I envy their freedom from clocks and calendars,
their immunity to pressure.

"Oh, they have their moments,
skinned knees and nap time,
but they recover quickly.
They don't nurse their disappointments
or make a career out of contrition.

"Lord,
kids are so neat!
Let me be converted
and become as a little child.

"Let me know again
the sheer joy of being alive, and
the pure pleasure
of living one day at a time,
fully savoring each solitary moment.

"Free me from past disappointments
and the little hurts
I've so carefully kept.

"Restore unto me
a childlike anticipation for life.
A sense of wonder
which makes each day new
and my life truly abundant."

"Recently a neighbor of ours took his two small children to the mountains for a vacation. The very first morning the children woke him at daybreak, clamoring to go exploring. Stifling an impulse to send them back to bed, he struggled into his clothes and took them for a walk. At the edge of a pond they stopped to rest and while they were sitting there quietly a doe and her fawn came down to drink.

" 'I watched my youngsters' faces,' he said, 'and suddenly it was as if I were seeing and feeling everything for the first time: the hush of the woods, the mist over the water, the grace and gentleness of those lovely creatures, the kinship of all living things. It only lasted a few seconds, but the thought came to me that happiness isn't something you have to strive and struggle for. It's simply an awareness of the beauty and harmony of existence. And I said to myself: Remember this moment, put it away carefully in your mind — because you may need to draw strength and comfort from it some day.' "5 Now that's play of a very rare and special kind; the kind from which memories are made.

Perhaps you've had an experience like that. I know I have. Just last summer we spent ten days vacationing in the Colorado Rockies. The mountains are always special to me, they never grow old. I love the crisp air scented with pine, the high meadows decked out like a huge bouquet of wildflowers, the soft whisper of the wind in the aspens, clear streams tumbling down the mountainside, noisy and icy cold, and sunsets painting snowcapped peaks in subtle hues. No matter how many times I experience it, I'm always moved.

But this time was extra special. Leah's boyfriend was with us and it was his first trip to the Rocky Mountains. By nature, Todd is one of the most inquisitive and enthusiastic people I've ever known. His love for life is absolutely contagious. Well, showing him the Rockies was like seeing them for the first time all over again. And like the aforementioned neighbor, I, too, realized that these were special moments to be cherished and relived through the passing years.

That trip and a vacation to Canada a year earlier didn't just happen. We had to plan and sacrifice for them. In fact, they grew out of a letter I wrote to Leah on March 13, 1985, while flying to Alaska to speak at a district men's retreat.

"Dear Leah:

"We are now about thirty minutes out of Seattle on the last leg of our flight to Anchorage. The weather is finally clear but it was real rough between Tulsa and Chicago and it was snowing when we landed at O'Hare. The Chicago airport is huge, the biggest one I've ever been in. We were late landing so I made like O.J. Simpson and ran to catch my connecting flight. Counting the three boxes of tapes and books plus my hanging bag, my suitcase, my briefcase and my camera bag, I had seven pieces of luggage. They would only let me check four pieces so I'm carrying my suitcase, briefcase and camera bag, plus my topcoat. Quite a load for an old man!"

There's a lot more, some special memories from across the years, some practical advice for the years to come and some things

I hope she will remember about me when she is grown with children of her own. And this:

"Leah, the last couple of years have been terribly busy, and I've missed you. In three years you will be off to college, and daddy's little girl will be gone. I don't want to waste your remaining years, so make a list of the things you would like us to do together, and then let's dedicate the next three years as one final fling at family time. Have your list ready when I get home and we'll get started."

At the top of her list was family vacations. Two of the places she wanted to go were Colorado and Canada. I turned most of the preliminary planning over to Brenda and Leah. They had great fun pouring over road maps as they mapped out our route and planned daily excursions. My fun is of a more practical kind — the vacation itself. Though I do have to admit that it seems I'm missing at least half the fun. They seem to get two vacations — the one they talk about and plan for weeks in advance, and the one we actually take.

I guess I'm trying to say that there are at least two kinds of family play: planned play — like vacations and other special events, and spontaneous play — those times when you simply seize the moment and live it for all it's worth. Don't let the terms confuse you. They both require planning and commitment. Play seldom just happens. You have to plan for it and make a commitment to fit it into your schedule. Maybe that's part of what Jim Elliot, the martyred missionary, meant when he wrote, "Wherever you are, be all there. Live to the hilt every situation you believe to be the will of God."[6] When it's time to play, when you're playing, play for all you are worth!

The temptation for committed men and women will always be to put off playing until a more opportune time. Beware! That's the deadliest of all traps. If you can't make time for play now, the chances are you never will. Busyness is not a temporary condition but a fact of life. The sooner we come to grips with that and commit to the rhythm of life — that delicate balance between work and rest, worship and play — the sooner we will consistently experience the Abundant Life. If we postpone play, I'm afraid we will awaken one day at the end of our lives to realize what we've missed. When that happens, the best we can hope for is the wistful regret so eloquently expressed by the anonymous friar who, late in his life, wrote:

"If I had my life to live over again, I'd try
   to make more mistakes next time.
I would relax, I would limber up, I would be sillier
   than I have been this trip.

"I know of very few things I would take seriously.
I would take more trips. I would be crazier.
I would climb more mountains, swim more rivers
   and watch more sunsets.
I would do more walking and looking.
I would eat more ice cream and less beans.
I would have more actual troubles, and fewer
   imaginary ones.

"You see, I'm one of those people who lives life
   prophylactically and sensibly hour after hour,
   day after day. Oh, I've had my moments, and if I
   had to do it over again I'd have more of them.
In fact, I'd try to have nothing else, just moments,
   one after another, instead of living so many
   years ahead each day. I've been one of those
   people who never go anywhere without a
   thermometer, a hot-water bottle, a gargle, a
   raincoat, aspirin, and a parachute.

"If I had to do it over again I would go places, do
   things, and travel lighter than I have.
If I had my life to live over I would start
   barefooted
   earlier in the spring and stay that way later in
   the fall.

I would play hooky more.
I wouldn't make such good grades, except by
  accident.
I would ride on more merry-go-rounds.
  I'd pick more daisies."[7]

In short, I think he's saying that, given another chance, he would play more!

Footnotes

1. Gordon Dahl, *Work, Play, And Worship In A Leisure-Oriented Society* (Minneapolis: Augsburg Publishing House, 1972), p. 12.

2. Norman Cousins, "Human Options," quoted in *Disciplines For The Inner Life,* p. 310.

3. Clyde Reid, "Celebrate the Temporary," quoted in *Disciplines For The Inner Life,* p. 331.

4. Joseph G. Donders, "The Tired Samaritan," quoted in *Christian Herald,* Apr. 1987, p. 45. (Reprinted in *Christian Herald* with permission from "Jesus, Hope Drawing Near" by Joseph G. Donders, published by Orbis).

5. Gordon, p. 153.

6. Swindoll, p. 214.

7. Hansel, pp. 44,45.

EPILOGUE

Even the most significant spiritual experiences, moments like Isaiah's vision in the temple or John the Beloved's encounter with the risen Christ on the Isle of Patmos, will be fleeting at best and of little lasting value unless they are reinforced with daily disciplines, ways of living which constantly remind us of His nearness and high calling.

Included in these disciplines, perhaps at their very heart, is what I've identified as the rhythm of life — that delicate balance between work and rest, worship and play. Without rhythm, the hardiest among us risk burnout, and life's richness hangs by a slender thread. Consider Elijah the prophet who had unparalleled spiritual experiences but who knew little or nothing of the abundant life or emotional wholeness until God gave him a crash course in the rhythm of life. After the spiritual and emotional high of Mount Carmel, Elijah crashed. God gave him forty days of enforced rest, a worship encounter that focused on relationships rather than power, a new commission and a special friend — Elisha. As a result, Elijah experienced spiritual wholeness and emotional stability.

Let me suggest that you add the rhythm of life to your spiritual disciplines. Meaningful work fulfills us as creative persons. Rest restores our physical energies, so we can work again. Worship renews us spiritually and gives definition and dimension to our lives. Play relieves the tension and gives balance to the whole of life. By divine design, we require it all, and we ignore this rhythm at our own peril.

Let me conclude with a prayer:

"Discipline is such a dirty word.
It creates pictures
of pain and self-denial.

"Freedom on the other hand
makes me think of
birds soaring in joyous flight,
children running on the beach
without a care in the world.

"Yet freedom without discipline
is not freedom at all.
It's permissiveness which leads to
the bondage of self-indulgence.

"The bird soaring in flight
is not 'free' from the laws of nature
but free to enjoy the disciplines
of flight based on those very laws.

"We are not 'free' from the rhythm of life,
rather we are free through the rhythm of life
to experience life to the very fullest.

"The disciplines of work and rest, worship and play,
are not a hair shirt to chafe us,
but a way of life which leads to perfect freedom:

"Freedom from unbridled ambition;
Freedom from self-centered restlessness;
Freedom from spiritual deadness.
Freedom from guilt.
Discipline — freedom indeed.

"Free to work and rest,
    worship and play!
Free to live and love,
    to sing and dance.
Free to become
    and to be!
Amen."

BIBLIOGRAPHY

BIBLIOGRAPHY

Allen, R. Earl. *Strength From Shadows*. Nashville: Broadman Press, 1967.

Allen, R. Earl. *Trials, Tragedies, and Triumphs*. Westwood: Fleming H. Revell, 1965.

Benson, Bob, and Benson, Michael W. *Disciplines For The Inner Life*. Waco: Word Books, 1985.

Bombeck, Erma. *At Wit's End*. Field Enterprises, Field Newspaper Syndicate, 1981.

Broderick, Carlfred. *Couples*. New York: Simon and Schuster, Inc., 1979.

Campolo, Anthony. *Who Switched the Price Tags?* Waco: Word Books, 1986.

Claypool, John. *Stages*. Waco: Word Books, 1977.

Cole, K. C. "Playing Together: From Couples That Play." *Psychology Today*. February 1982.

Collins, Gary. *You Can Profit From Stress*. Santa Ana: Vision House, 1977.

Dahl, Gordon. *Work, Play and Worship In A Leisure-Oriented Society*. Minneapolis: Augsburg Publishing House, 1972.

Dobson, James C. *Straight Talk to Men and Their Wives*. Waco: Word Books, 1980.

Donders, Joseph G. "The Tired Samaritan." *Christian Herald*. April 1987.

Exley, Richard D. *The Other God.* Plainfield: Logos International, 1979.

Foster, Richard. *The Freedom of Simplicity.* San Francisco: Harper & Row, 1981.

Goldberg, Alan D. "The Sabbath: Implications for Mental Health." *Counseling and Values.* April 1987.

Gordon, Arthur. *A Touch of Wonder.* Old Tappan: Spire Books, Fleming H. Revell, 1974.

Guisewite, Cathy. "Cathy." United Press Syndicate, 1987. *The Tulsa World,* 3 March 1987.

Hansel, Tim. *When I Relax I Feel Guilty.* Elgin: David C. Cook, 1979.

Hembree, Charles. *Pocket of Pebbles.* Grand Rapids: Baker Book House, 1969.

Hirsch, S. R. *HOREB: A Philosophy of Jewish Laws and Observances.* New York: Soncino, 1962.

Irion, Mary Jean. "Gift From A Hair Dryer." *United Church Herald.* November 1962. Reprinted in *Yes, World: A Mosaic of Meditation.* Richard W. Baron, 1970.

James, G. Robert. *Michael.* An unpublished work.

Kazantzakis, Nikos. *Zorba The Greek.* New York: Ballatine Books, 1952.

Killinger, John. *For God's Sake, Be Human.* Waco: Word Books, 1970.

Kreitler, Peter, and Bruns, Bill. *Affair Prevention.* New York: Macmillan, 1981.

Kushner, Harold. *When All You've Ever Wanted Isn't Enough.* New York: Summit Books — A Division of Simon and Schuster, Inc., 1986.

Larson, Bruce. *The Relational Revolution.* Waco: Word Books, 1976.

Lindstrom, Aletha Jane. "A Legacy of Rainbows." *Reader's Digest,* December 1984.

MacDonald, Gordon. *Ordering Your Private World.* Nashville: Published by a Division of Thomas Nelson, 1984.

MacDonald, Gordon. *Restoring Your Spiritual Passion.* Nashville: Oliver Nelson, a Division of Thomas Nelson, 1986.

McKenna, David L. *The Communicator's Commentary: Mark.* Waco: Word Books, 1982.

McNamara, William. "Wasting Time Creatively" (cassette tape), Spiritual Life Institute, Star Route One, Sedona, Arizona.

"Midlife Crisis — Is It Avoidable?" *U.S. News & World Report*, 25 October, 1982.

Miles, C. Austin. "In The Garden." *Hymns of Glorious Praise.* Springfield: Gospel, 1969.

Muto, Susan A. *Pathways Of Spiritual Living.* Garden City: Doubleday & Company, Inc., 1984.

Oates, Wayne E. *Nurturing Silence In a Noisy Heart.* Garden City: Doubleday & Company, Inc., 1979.

Oatman Jr., Johnson, and Hugg, George C. "No Not One!" *Hymns of Glorious Praise.* Springfield: Gospel, 1969.

Osler, William. *Familiar Quotations.* Boston: Little, Brown and Company, 1955.

Prather, Hugh. *I Touch The Earth, The Earth Touches Me.* Garden City: Doubleday & Company, Inc., 1972.

Raines, Robert. *Creative Brooding.* New York: Macmillan, 1966.

Ruch, Floyd L., and Zimbardo, Philip G. *Psychology And Life.* 8th Ed. Glenview: Scott, Foresman and Company, 1971.

Sanders, J. Oswald. *Spiritual Leadership.* Chicago: Moody Press, 1967.

Scriven, Joseph, and Converse, Charles C. "What A Friend We Have In Jesus." *Hymns of Glorious Praise.* Springfield: Gospel, 1969.

Shedd, Charlie W. *Letters To Phillip: On How To Treat A Woman.* Garden City: Doubleday & Company, Inc., 1968.

Speakman, Frederick B. *The Salty Tang.* Westwood: Fleming H. Revell.

Swindoll, Charles R. *Growing Strong In The Seasons Of Life.* Portland: Multnomah Press, 1983.

"Taking Time," U.S. Department of Health and Human Services, *NIH Publication No. 82-2059.* September 1982.

Thatcher, Floyd W. *The Splendor of Easter.* Waco: Word Books, 1980.

Thigpen, Paul. "Dad, Are We Having Fun Yet?" *Charisma,* June 1987.

Toplady, Augustus M., and Hastings, Thomas. "Rock of Ages." *Hymns of Glorious Praise.* Springfield: Gospel, 1969.

Viorst, Judith. *How Did I Get To Be 40 & Other Atrocities.* New York: Simon and Schuster, Inc., 1978.

Wright, H. Norman. *Seasons of a Marriage.* Ventura: Regal Books — a Division of Gospel Light Publications, 1982.